ANATOMY OF FITNESS
501
Core Exercises

hinkler

Published by Hinkler Books Pty Ltd 2018
45–55 Fairchild Street
Heatherton Victoria 3202 Australia
www.hinkler.com

hinkler

Created by Moseley Road Inc.
Cover Designer: Sam Grimmer
Prepress: Splitting Image
Production Director: Adam Moore
Designer: Kate Stretton
Photographer: Naila Ruechel
Author: Natasha Diamond-Walker

ISBN: 978 1 4889 3404 9

Printed and bound in China

GENERAL DISCLAIMER

The contents of this book are intended to provide useful information to the general public. All materials, including texts, graphics, and images, are for informational purposes only and are not a substitute for medical diagnosis, advice, or treatment for specific medical conditions. All readers should seek expert medical care and consult their own physicians before commencing any exercise program or for any general or specific health issues. The author and publishers do not recommend or endorse specific treatments, procedures, advice, or other information found in this book and specifically disclaim all responsibility for any and all liability, loss, or risk, personal or otherwise, which is incurred as a consequence, directly or indirectly, of the use or application of any of the material in this publication.

ANATOMY OF FITNESS™
501
Core Exercises

Craft perfect workouts for your own training goals
and discover the amazing hidden structure of your body

Contents

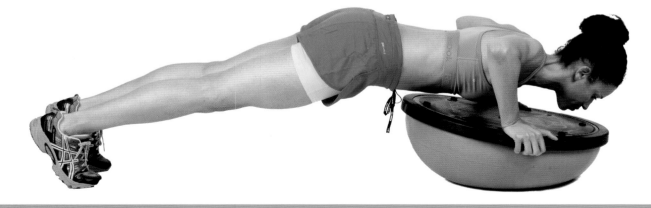

Introduction

What is the core?

When it comes to fitness and working out, we often hear a lot about the core. But, really, what do they mean when they say "core?" It sounds mysterious and a little bit hard to place, if you think about it. For starters, we can assume that the core is located in the center somewhere; after all, the core of a peach is at its center. So, we have an idea of where it is, but a little information about what it is, exactly, would be nice. To put it simply, when we refer to the "core" we are talking about the centers of our bodies. In fitness, it is commonly understood that the core encompasses all of the abdominal muscle groups, the middle and lower back muscles, and, in most cases, the pelvis as well. Core-based workouts are plentiful and often focus on routines based around working the abdominals. Our cores are important, because in order to support optimal function throughout the rest of the body, our cores must be healthy and strong.

Your healthy spine

In order to live a healthy life, we need a healthy spinal column to support our bones, muscles, and organs. Made up of 33 individual bones interconnected with our nervous system, our spines and our spinal health dictate much of our day-to-day lives. The spine traverses more than 50 percent of our body's length and contains over 120 muscles and 100 joints, alone. So, when you move through your workout and daily activities, remember to thank your spine for all its support!

Let's talk back

Moving on from the spine and all of its fun facts, we should discuss the back. When we say "back," we are using a blanket term for the total area that makes up the distance from the shoulders, down to the backbone or sacrum. The muscles of the middle back and the lower back are all supported by the spine, at the most deep level, and then by the muscles that make up the core, on a more superficial level. Our backs are responsible for carrying a lot of weight and, thus, require a sufficient amount of attention, development, and care. When you are formatting your workouts, take time to include exercises that strengthen your back so that it may be healthy, pain free, and reliable.

Eat up

What to eat, what to eat, what to eat. So much talk about diet! And not to mention losing weight, gaining weight, organic, holistic, vegan, vegetarian, gluten-free this, sugar-free that, and Paleo. Honestly—all fun aside—your diet, and what you choose or don't choose to put into your body is important. If you intend to have a successful life of working out, feeling good, and living up to your best potential, you should take care to develop a sustainable diet that works best for you and your individual needs. Information abounds via the internet about all things diet-related. It is a great resource for researching and planning a lifestyle that suits you fully.

The Pilates influence

Joseph Pilates once said that "A man is as young as his spine is strong." He was a profound individual who believed in living your best life by way of taking care of your physical body. Pilates felt that if you took good care of your physical body, you would inevitably manifest good feelings and happiness in all other parts of your life. He is solely responsible for what we now know as "Pilates." Developing a system of movements that are centered around strengthening the back, core, and pelvis, Joseph Pilates goes down in history as one of the most prolific people to influence the great wide world of fitness today.

Yoga and fitness

If you have ever done yoga in your life, you know that it can be quite dynamic. With the holds, and the breathing, and the sweating, and putting your leg somewhere you thought it could never go, it is a challenge, to say the least. However challenging it may be, it is a wonderful craft to incorporate into your workout routines. Pairing yoga and other styles of aerobic activity is highly rewarding and fulfilling. By performing different levels of yoga moves, you will teach the body to breathe deeper, to open more, and to find balance both inside and outside of yourself.

Props on top of props

The vast abundant world of props! You might be thinking that you do not need to include props in any of your workouts, and you are right—you don't! But if you do, your exercise results could far exceed what you even dreamed possible. Incorporating props into your workout regime can be fun, challenging, and highly aerobic. The great thing about using props is that they add all sorts of dimensions into your moves. For example, planking on the floor is great. However, planking with your hands centered on a balance ball, while holding a dumbbell in one hand out to the side, will invite the muscles to work in a whole new way! Some of the props you will find utilized in this book are resistance bands, cables, balance balls, kettlebells, dumbbells, Medicine Balls, Swiss balls, and step platforms.

Stay home or hit the gym?

Whether you choose to work out at home or to work out at the gym, either way, you are choosing the path of bettering your health. Both are good options that provide different benefits, depending on what type of gym or home workout system you have in place. Some people find it useful to get up and go out to a public space, like a gym. The idea that there are other people in a joint setting, doing the same things in the pursuit of wellness, is inspiring to them. While others enjoy the privacy of their own homes to exercise in. Or they are just unable to attend the gym because of money or time restrictions. It is your personal choice which you choose, of course. However, with the publication of books like this one, online workout routines, and the ability to pick up just about any sort of exercise prop at the store, working out at home has become just as simple as hitting the gym!

Plyometric play

You will see the use of the word "plyometric" sprinkled throughout this book, as you move through crafting your routines. A plyometric exercise is defined as a quick, powerful movement that starts with a muscle lengthening (eccentric) movement that is immediately followed by a muscle shortening (concentric) movement. Or, more simply, you can think of it as jump training. Plyometric exercises require you to move quickly into your range in a short amount of time, but with the maximum amount of speed and power. Incorporating plyometric exercises 1 to 3 times a week can increase your muscle tone and strength, as well as allow you to move more quickly and powerfully.

Getting organized

So, here you are, you have the book in hand, you have thought about your diet and what parts of your physique you would like to chisel out and strengthen—what next? The next thing that needs to be sorted out is what kind of routine you are going to set up. Some things to keep in mind are what your work schedule is like, how much time you would like to spend exercising, what times of day you have the most energy, whether you would like a personal trainer, and if you think working out at home versus the gym is a good choice for you. Planning your work and working your plan are two major parts on the path to health and wellness. You are here now, so let's get started!

Why exercise?

There is so much talk nowadays, more than ever, about working out. Everyone seems to be getting their Hollywood bodies handcrafted by doctors, joining shiny fads of monster cycling, or signing up for those acrobatic pole-dance cardio classes. But, truly, what does it really mean to work out? To exercise, to take interest in your health and wellness? Well, the meaning of what it is to work out is definitely personal and individual to each of us. Whether you are someone who enjoys an intense sweaty one-hour heavy lifting session, or you prefer short bursts of cardio coupled with a yoga cooldown, take care to spend time crafting your need-specific workout routine. And feel free to mix it up a little bit as you go, trying different moves and tempos along the way.

Moving with your breath

Whether the focus of your workouts is to put on muscle mass, to lose weight, to tone, to feel better, or to gain flexibility, all require you to have an optimal flow of breath. Breathing is so important when it comes to working out. There are so many ways to breathe, and discovering the right pairing of breath with each exercise is a personal journey. However, you should keep in mind that breathing regulates the oxygen flow throughout the body. This includes oxygen in the lungs and also to and from the muscles. For optimal workout results you must remember to breathe deeply and frequently, usually inhaling at the beginning of a movement and exhaling as you move.

Full-Body Anatomy

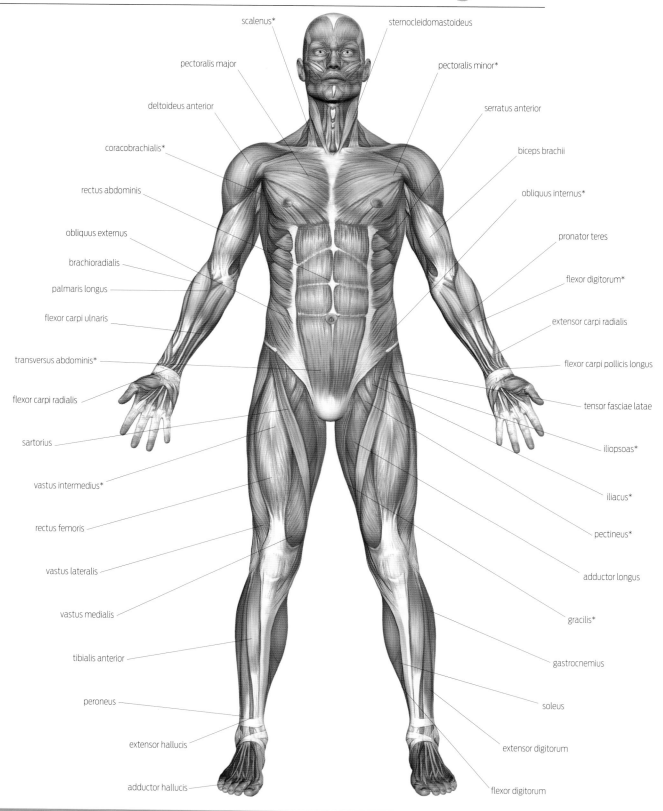

scalenus*

sternocleidomastoideus

pectoralis major

pectoralis minor*

deltoideus anterior

serratus anterior

coracobrachialis*

biceps brachii

rectus abdominis

obliquus internus*

obliquus externus

pronator teres

brachioradialis

flexor digitorum*

palmaris longus

extensor carpi radialis

flexor carpi ulnaris

transversus abdominis*

flexor carpi pollicis longus

flexor carpi radialis

tensor fasciae latae

sartorius

iliopsoas*

vastus intermedius*

iliacus*

rectus femoris

pectineus*

vastus lateralis

adductor longus

vastus medialis

gracilis*

tibialis anterior

gastrocnemius

peroneus

soleus

extensor hallucis

extensor digitorum

adductor hallucis

flexor digitorum

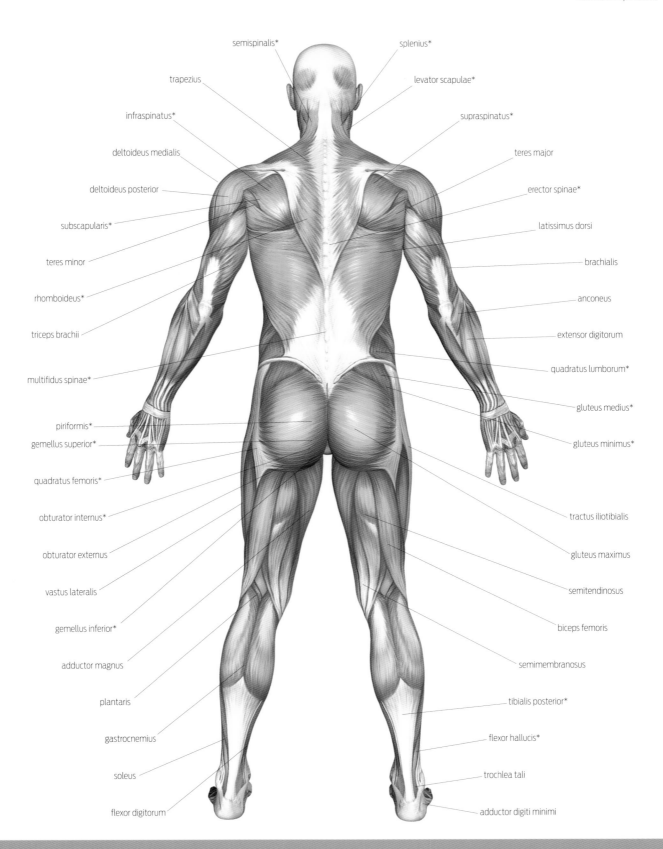

semispinalis*

splenius*

trapezius

levator scapulae*

infraspinatus*

supraspinatus*

deltoideus medialis

teres major

deltoideus posterior

erector spinae*

subscapularis*

latissimus dorsi

teres minor

brachialis

rhomboideus*

anconeus

triceps brachii

extensor digitorum

multifidus spinae*

quadratus lumborum*

piriformis*

gluteus medius*

gemellus superior*

gluteus minimus*

quadratus femoris*

obturator internus*

tractus iliotibialis

obturator externus

gluteus maximus

vastus lateralis

semitendinosus

gemellus inferior*

biceps femoris

adductor magnus

semimembranosus

plantaris

tibialis posterior*

gastrocnemius

flexor hallucis*

soleus

trochlea tali

flexor digitorum

adductor digiti minimi

CHAPTER ONE

Dynamic Exercises

Our bodies are magnificent creations, made up of all sorts of tissues, organs, muscles, and bones. Each system works with the next to keep us in balance and functioning at our best. Generally, when looking into fitness routines, we pinpoint a specific area that we would like to work on, and choose the best workouts to match. These dynamic exercises are intended to enhance core power and strength. As you move through the dynamic exercise routines found in this book, you will discover that when you focus on developing core power, you simultaneously boost stability in every other part of the body.

Dynamic Exercises

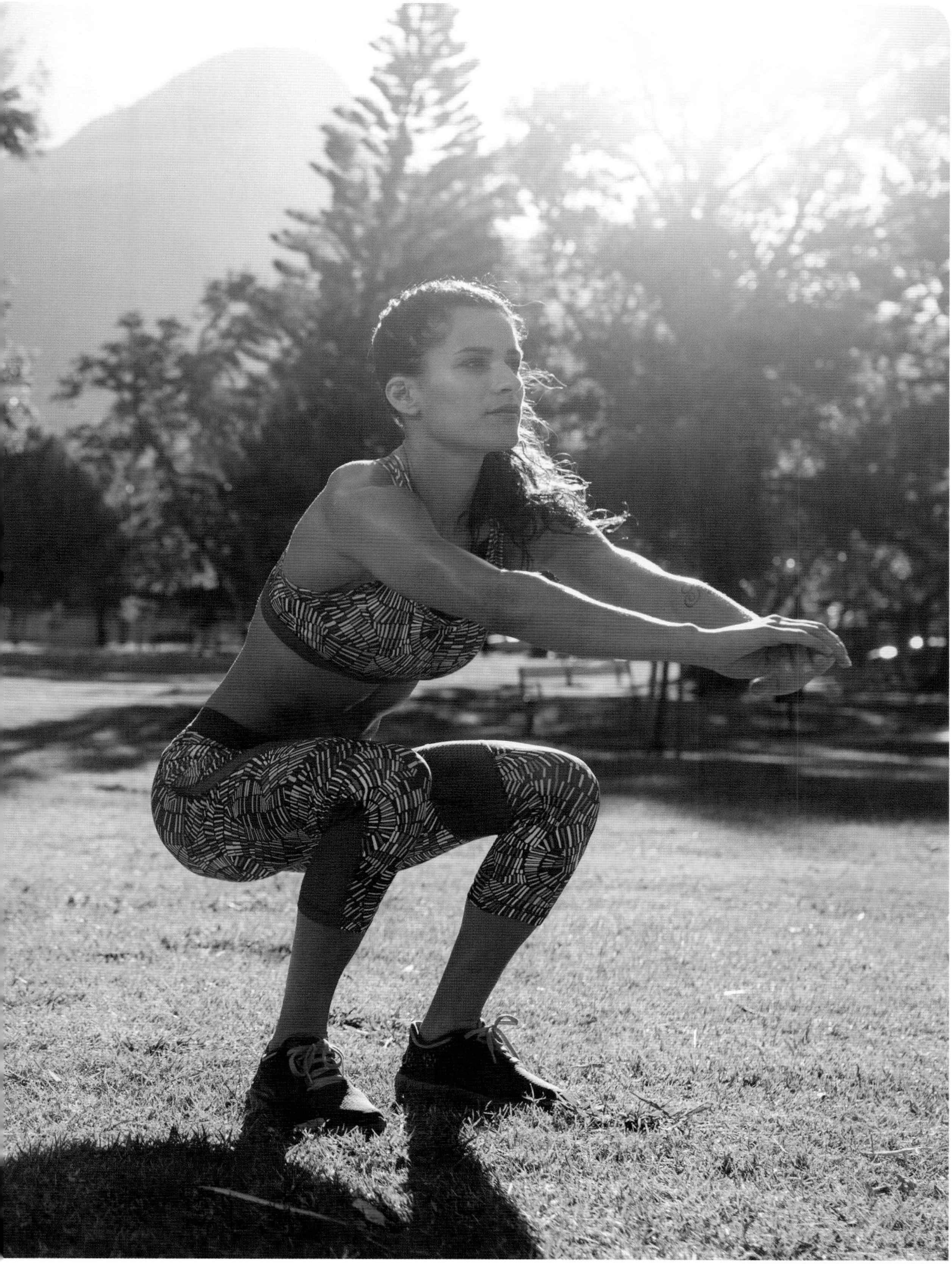

001

Basic Squat

The squat is a common exercise that many of us perform every day without too much thought, from bending down to tie a shoe to picking up a small child. However, when added into a workout routine and done with deliberate intention, this Basic Squat movement can powerfully strengthen and shape the abdominal core, lower back, and legs. It is a pretty straightforward move that requires perfect square alignment from the top of the head to the base of the foot, striving for each joint to be stacked and supported on top of each other in a straight line. The better your form, the better your results will be!

gluteus medius*
gluteus maximus
tensor fasciae latae
vastus lateralis
biceps femoris

rectus abdominis
vastus intermedius
rectus femoris
sartorius
vastus medialis
gastrocnemius
adductor magnus

Correct form

In your squat, knees should stay at a 90-degree angle to your hips. You should feel the work and weight in your quads and hamstrings with the abdominals working to stay up and into the back.

Avoid

Do not bring the upper body too far forward. Hold your abs in strongly and allow your spine to stay on a diagonal.

- Stand with your feet shoulder width apart, about a foot and a half (50 cm) distance, and your knees evenly under your hips. Your hips should be square on top of your legs. Shift your weight so that it is poised over the balls of your feet, toward your toes.
- Lift your arms, with palms down, and reach forward through your fingertips out front.
- Bend your knees so that they track smoothly above your ankles. Keep your heels rooted as you descend. The hips will hinge back, bringing the entire shape of your torso slightly forward.
- Slowly lift back up to stand.

002 Static Sumo Squat

Open your legs wide and turn your feet out with your hands on each thigh. Lengthen your spine with abdominals pulled up, and bend deeply at the knees. Once thighs reach a 90-degree angle to the knee, return to standing.

003 Split Squat

Be sure to start in a wide open stance with the legs comfortably far apart from each other. The further apart, the longer the muscle you build.

- In a staggered stance, bend both knees into 90-degree angles, parallel to the ground. Keep abdominals tucked into the spine and knees over ankles. Straighten the front leg and return to standing. Switch legs. Feel the burn!

- Keep your abdominals strongly engaged the whole time. Have the feeling that your abs are pulling in toward your spine.

- Don't put too much strain into the lower back and keep the back muscles long and strong.

004 Dumbbell Split Squat

With dumbbells take a staggered stance. Descend into a Split Squat (#003) and quickly return to standing. Keep arms glued at sides. Adding speed when returning to stand with dumbbells will create quicker muscle response and better balance throughout the body. Switch legs and repeat.

005 Split Squat with Band Row

In a Split Squat stance (#003) hold the band in both hands firmly with resistance. Now, squat, pulling the band into your body, bending the elbows, engaging the backs of the arms. With control and working against the band, return to standing. Repeat with the other leg in front.

006

Overhead Sandbag Split Squat

Standing with one foot in front of the other—sandbag in hands—bend your front knee, raising the sandbag up over your head. Challenge your core and leg muscles to work a little deeper! Return to standing, lowering the bag. Repeat with the other leg in front.

007

Split Squat with Band Curl

Place a band under the front foot, keeping a good grip on the band. Lower into a squat, arms glued to sides. Bending at the elbows, pull the band up toward the shoulders, working the front of the arms. Then stand, keeping resistance on the band. Switch legs and repeat.

008

Squat Thrust

This variation combines both a squat and a plank. Working isometrically, you will develop the ability to move with quick bursts of energy, stimulating the muscles of the body to work in a more dynamic way.

- With feet apart and under your hips, raise the arms.
- In one move crouch down, hands to the floor. Explode out into a plank. Quickly return to the crouched position.
- Last, fling the arms up to the sky, standing tall with energy.

009

Side Bend Squat

With legs wide and toes turned out, squeeze your core and bend at the knees. Hold it there! Open the arms, engage your side abs, and reach one hand toward your ankle with the other up to the sky. Stand and repeat on the other side!

Side Expansion

Side bending in any exercise is a great way to open up and lengthen the outer parts of the torso and the muscles that run along the spine. Bending to the side is also a stretch for the lungs, allowing more space to expand and breathe deeply.

010

Pistol Squat

In Basic Squat stance (#001), lift the right leg off the ground. With the leg raised, tip the hips back, and lower slowly into a squat. Take care of your bending knee by strongly engaging the abs the whole time! Swap legs and repeat.

011

Single Leg Piriformis Squat with Forward Reach

Reach the arms front and place the left ankle on top of the right knee. Squeeze your glutes and squat, stretching your left knee open against the right leg. Let the hips push back while the arms reach forward in opposition! Swap legs and repeat.

012 Suspended Single Leg Squat

This variation of the Pistol Squat enhances the movement stretch by holding on to straps. Hold a strap in each hand and descend into the squat position. Use the straps for a deeper squat stretch. Swap legs and repeat.

013 Bulgarian Split Squat

Start in a well staggered position, back leg elevated on a bench or step. Squat with both knees bent, feeling the front of the back hip lengthen and stretch. Switch legs and add hand weights as you wish!

014 Bulgarian Split Squat with Swiss Ball

Put the top of your foot onto the Swiss ball and stabilize your standing leg by activating your core and hamstrings. Lower into a squat, making sure your knee and extended leg are in one line parallel to the floor. Swap legs.

015 Swiss Ball Bulgarian Split Squat with Overhead Press

Put the top of one foot onto the Swiss ball and stabilize your standing leg by activating your core and hamstrings. Press your arms slowly overhead and lower into a squat. Switch legs and repeat. Keep your abs pulled in strongly!

016 Bulgarian Split Squat with Overhead Dumbbell Press

Combining your Split Squat with an overhead press adds an element of upper arm weight work. Pushing the dumbbells up with the arms while lowering the body into the squat is a great way to work the extremities in two directions at once.

- Get into a Bulgarian Split Squat stance (#013) with your arms at your sides, dumbbells in hands.
- As you squat, isolate the elbows to bend and then press up overhead. Keep your spine straight and shoulders down.
- Push down into your front leg, pull in the abs, straighten your front leg, and return to standing. Repeat with the other leg in front.

017 Bulgarian Split Squat with Disc Weight

Take your Split Squat stance (#003) with the back foot elevated. Suspend your weighted disc in front of your chest, firmly squeezing in your abs. Lower into your squat, keeping the disc there. Hold! Return to standing. Repeat with the other leg in front.

018 Bulgarian Split Squat with Disc Twist Variation

In Bulgarian Split Squat stance (#013), hold the disc to your chest. Squat deeply and hold there. Keep your hips facing front and spiral the upper abs and shoulders to one side. Extend the disc out for an added challenge! Repeat with the other leg in front.

019 Chair Plié

Stand behind a chair with wide open legs, toes turned out. Keeping your core up and in along your spine, bend at the knees until your toes and knees are aligned, making a 90-degree angle. Inhale and return to standing.

020 Side Leaning Sumo Squat

Take your sumo squat and hold deeply at the bottom of it. Engage your glutes, hamstrings, and abs. Place one hand to your knee, extending the other arm up high and then over to your side. Stretch and hold here! Straighten and repeat on the other side.

021 Toe Touch Sumo Squat

Go into your sumo squat with hands on thighs. In one move, bend forward and touch your toes, stretching your lower back and stabilizing your core and lower leg muscle groups. Stand and repeat.

022 Toe Touch Sumo Squat with Reach

Perform your best sumo squat with hands on thighs. Hold at the bottom. Move your hands forward to your toes. Hold. Spiral open your chest to one side, reaching your arm up along your side to the sky. Reverse and repeat!

023 Battle Rope Full Squat Alternating Waves

With a battle rope in each hand, stand with the legs open. Bend into a full squat for balance and squeeze your arms into the sides of your body. Vigorously alternate arm waves with battle ropes, engaging your core strongly!

024 Battle Rope Jump Squat and Slam

With battle ropes in hand, take your Basic Squat stance (#001). Lower to squat and once at the bottom of your bend, explode up into a jump with straight legs, flinging your ropes up, and then slam back down into a squat!

025 Balance Beam Single Leg Squat

Find your balance on the beam by pulling in the abs, lengthening the spine, and engaging your leg muscles. With arms in front of you for added balance, lift one leg and lower slowly into a squat. Squeeze your glutes! Switch legs and repeat.

026 Trampoline Squat

Do your Basic Squat on the trampoline in this variation! For added fun, try an explosive jump up from the bottom of your squat! This variation enhances core balance by playing with an unstable base.

- Stand tall with both feet together and arms relaxed at your sides. Be sure you are in the center of the trampoline.
- Bend the knees deeply and then spring up into the air. Engage your legs and abs.
- Land in your squat position with the arms reaching out in front of you.

Trampoline Perks

Adding a trampoline into your workouts gives you greater range of motion for jumping and bending. It also enhances the stretch of the claves, ankles, and feet when taking off and landing. Be sure to always stabilize your extremities from the core when on the trampoline.

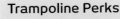

027 Trampoline Triple Squat Lateral Step-Up

With knees bent, arms open, start with your right foot on the trampoline. Take a squat, step the left foot up to meet the right, stabilize both feet, step the right foot off to the right, then the left! Reverse and repeat.

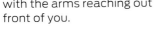

028 Medicine Ball Single Leg Squat

For this squat assume your Pistol Squat position (#010) with a Medicine ball in hand. Challenging your balance, squat down with one leg extended in front. Smoothly rise to stand. For more difficulty, try this on the balance beam! Repeat with the other leg raised.

029 Weighted Ball Power Squat

Stand on one leg, holding the weighted ball above your shoulder. In one move squat down, sweeping the ball across the body, then stand, lifting the ball back up. Switch legs and repeat. Completing this sequence quickly develops lateral core and glute power!

030 Medicine Ball Split Squat

Holding the Medicine ball out in front, take a staggered stance. Descend into Split Squat (#003) and quickly return to standing. Keep the arms forward. Switch legs and repeat. Straightening quickly will create faster muscle response and better balance throughout the body.

031 Weighted Ball Sumo Squat with Overhead Lift

Take your sumo squat stance, holding the weighted ball high overhead. Lengthen your spine with abdominals pulled up, bend deeply at the knees, lowering the ball and engaging the back. Once your thighs reach a 90-degree angle to your knees, return to standing.

032 Wall Squat

Stand against a wall. Walk your feet out about 1.5 feet (50 cm). With arms at shoulder level, feet hip width apart, squat down, keeping your back against the wall, until your knees reach a 90-degree angle. Hold it there!

033 Wall Squat with Bicep Curl

Working with your weight supported by a wall behind you allows you to deeply stabilize your core while also engaging the legs. Think of pressing into the surface behind you the entire time, giving your back muscles a stretch.

- Stand against the wall with dumbbells in each hand.
- Standing tall, reach the arms out in front of you at chest height, palms facing upward.
- Hug the elbows in and isolate the bend of your arms into a 90-degree angle while you squat.
- Hold a moment at the bottom of your squat, then rise to standing again.

Wall Talk

When you use a wall for your squats, you allow your spine to work in its most perfect alignment. Pressing against the wall gives you the opportunity to elongate your spine and traction out the verterbra, gaining a very nice stretch.

034 Swiss Ball Wall Squat

Engage your abs and balance standing against a Swiss ball with your arms straight out in front of you. With a straight spine and the legs active, bend slowly into a squat, keeping pressure on the ball. Pull the abs up and in to stand!

035 Swiss Ball Wall Squat with Bicep Curl

Balanced along a Swiss ball, squat with dumbbells in each hand. Hug the elbows in and isolate the bend of your arms while you squat. Hold at the bottom and repeat! Keep resistance in your legs and spine!

036 Swiss Ball Single Leg Wall Squat with Bicep Curl

Go for your Swiss Ball Wall Squat with Bicep Curl (#035), but with one leg off the ground. Your standing leg will need to work much harder to keep the knee aligned over the toes! Pull in those abs and lower up and down with ease. Switch legs and repeat.

037

Basic Forward Lunge

The forward lunge comes in many variations, shapes, and sizes. It can be found in numerous movement systems including yoga, cross-training, classical dance, football, baseball, tennis, and mixed martial arts, just to name a few. It is a powerful movement that allows you to push and pull in a variety of directions all at once—forward, backward, side, up, and down into gravity.

Correct form
Pull the core muscles up and in to lengthen along the spine. Let the head float on top of the neck and put the weight of your feet forward into your toes.

Avoid
Don't bend the back leg. Keep it straight with the heel slightly off the ground. Try not to let it sway.

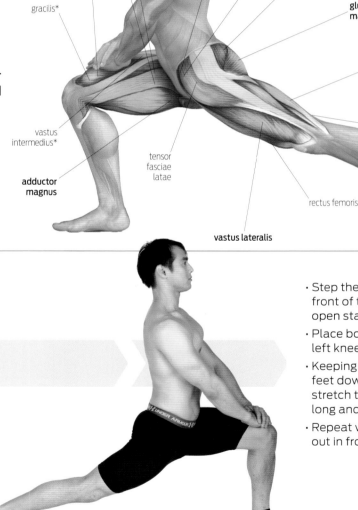

adductor brevis
adductor longus
vastus medialis
gracilis*
vastus intermedius*
adductor magnus
iliopsoas*
pectineus*
gluteus minimus*
gluteus maximus
biceps femoris
semitendinosus
tensor fasciae latae
rectus femoris
vastus lateralis

- Step the left foot out in front of the right in a wide open staggered stance.
- Place both hands on the left knee and bend deeply.
- Keeping both balls of the feet down into the floor, stretch the back leg out long and straight.
- Repeat with the right leg out in front.

038 Low Lunge

Take your forward lunge and place your hands on the floor to either side of your bent knee. Look down at your hands, pushing the back heel far back. Breathe. This is a deep leg stretch! Stand and repeat with the other leg in front.

039 Low Lunge with Reach

In all lunges it is very important to keep the front bent leg at a stable distance from the forward foot. You want your knee to be over the ankle when bent. Do not push the weight of the body down into the hips and lower back. Instead reach up and out toward your arms.

- Move into a forward lunge. Place both hands together overhead in a prayer position.
- Open the chest forward and up, bringing your gaze above you toward your hands.
- Breathe deeply and squeeze the core in to strengthen the back!
- Repeat with the other leg in front.

040 Dumbbell Lunge

Stand tall with dumbbells at each side. Keeping the abs tucked in and spine long, step forward into a lunge. Take care to keep the forward knee over the ankle at a 90-degree angle. Step quickly back to stand. Switch legs and repeat.

041 Lateral Lunge

With feet together and arms in front, take a big step to the left, bending the left knee and lengthening the right leg. Keep the back straight up and core tight. Spring off the left foot to stand as you began. Switch legs and repeat.

042 Reverse Lunge and Kick

Standing with hands on hips, step back into a lunge with both legs bent. Kick off the back leg, extending that leg straight out in front and swinging the arms in opposition. Land back again with both legs bent. Swap legs and repeat

043 Skater's Lunge

Many athletes incorporate this variation of lunge into their workouts because of its ability to work the leg muscles on a deep lateral plane. Additionally, you give your hamstrings and lower back a stretch when in the lunge position.

Lunge for Your Life

Lunges are one of the most simple moves to do. They are excellent for building up those inner and outer leg muscles that provide stability for your back. Lunges are also excellent for improving posture and balance, and stretching the hamstrings and calves.

- Standing with your feet shoulder-width apart, lean forward and place both hands on your right thigh.
- Lunge forward and right, bending your elbows.
- Angle your back over the bent knee with a straight spine.
- Spring off the supporting foot to stand as you began.
- Repeat on the opposite side.

044 Walking Lunge

Performing walking lunges and lower body workouts is a sure way to create better balance and coordination. The nervous system and spine are stabilized through balance work too. By pulling up the core and activating the larger leg muscle groups, you strengthen the whole body.

- Stand tall and step forward generously with one leg into your lunge.
- With both legs bent and hands on your hips, spring up to standing tall as you began.
- Alternate legs and repeat as if you were walking normally for as long as you can.

045 Single Leg Lateral Lunge and Lift

Step into a Lateral Lunge (#041) with your right foot and arms pointing downward. Straighten your right leg, lifting the left leg up. Re-bend the right leg into a Lateral Lunge. Take care to hold your core tight! Swap legs and repeat.

046 Switch Lunge

Step into a deep lunge with your right foot, arms extended behind. Hop up and quickly switch legs, landing in a deep lunge with your right leg forward.

047 Twisting Lunge

Stand tall and step forward generously with one leg into your lunge. With both legs bent, twist, reaching one hand to your inner ankle and the other up to the sky. Open the chest and breathe deeply. Swap legs and repeat.

048 Diagonal Lunge

Start upright with a long spine, feet together, hands on hips. Tighten your core into your back, pivot your feet to the diagonal, and take a large step out. Quickly return to standing, working the inner and outer legs! Repeat, alternating the lunging leg.

049 Forward Lunge with Twist

Take your forward lunge and place one hand on the floor inside the bent knee. Open the chest and swing open your other arm. Breathe. This is a chest and leg stretch! Stand and repeat to the other side.

050 Forward Lunge with Rear Leg Lift

With hands on hips, step forward into a lunge with both legs bent. Kick off the back leg, extending the leg straight out behind you. Land with both legs bent. Swap legs and repeat. This is great for defining the legs!

051 Balance Ball Forward Lunge

Executing the Balance Ball Forward Lunge correctly requires the ability to lengthen the front of the hips and the legs. When done in combination with other exercises, the lunge can become a powerful catalyst for body awareness and developing lower body strength.

- Start with feet slightly apart, arms front.
- In one move, step into a lunge on the balance ball bending your right leg.
- Quickly push off the balance ball and step back to stand. Swap legs and repeat. Using the balance ball works the hamstring deeply!

052 Balance Ball Side Lunge

With feet together and arms front, take a big lateral step to the right onto the balance ball, bending the right knee and lengthening the left leg. Keep your spine long! Spring off the right foot to stand as you began. Swap sides and repeat.

053 Balance Ball Static Lunge with Ball Throw

Holding the ball against the chest, keeping abs tucked in and spine long, step forward into a lunge on balance ball. Take care to keep the forward knee over the ankle. Toss the ball up, with balance, and catch again! Repeat with the other leg in front.

054 Forward Lunge with Weighted Ball Pass Under

Step generously forward into a deep lunge with both legs bent and the weighted ball against the chest. Hold the lunge and quickly pass the ball under the forward leg, isolating the movement of the arms and working the core for balance. Repeat with the other leg in front.

055 Lunge with Overhead Medicine Ball Press

Holding the ball against the chest, lift the right leg up and hold for a count, step forward into a lunge with both legs bent, raising the ball overhead. With balance, push back up onto a straight leg. Repeat, starting on the other leg.

056 Balance Beam Forward Lunge

Start with one foot in front of the other, arms out for balance. Take your forward lunge and bend the back knee so that it lightly touches the balance beam. Slowly, come to stand, and drag the front leg in. Repeat, starting with the other foot in front!

057 Front Lunge Pass Under

Step generously forward into a deep lunge with both legs bent and Medicine ball against the chest. Tilt the torso forward and quickly pass the ball under the forward leg, isolating the movement of the arms and working the core for balance. Switch legs and repeat.

058 Single Leg Lateral Lunge and Lift with Dumbbell

When your take your Lateral Lunge (#041), it is important to make sure that the bent knee is tracking straight over your heel. Do not let the hips rock back when you bend into your lunge. Keep your back on the diagonal and pull your core in strongly.

Shape and Sculpt

If you are looking to tone the upper leg and glute muscles, lunges are an excellent way to do that. By isolating your hip and knee joints into a bent position, you focus the work of the body into the legs. This produces sculpted and toned thighs, quads, hamstrings, and buttocks!

- Step into a Lateral Lunge (#041) on your right leg.
- Frame your bent knee with the dumbbells, stay there, and straighten your right leg, lifting the spine and left leg up. Lunge again.
- Repeat on the other side! Take care to hold your core tight!

059 Reverse Lunge

The opposite of your forward lunge is the Reverse Lunge. Stand tall with feet together, step back behind yourself into a lunge with both legs bent. Keep your back straight and your body weight forward and balanced! Repeat, stepping back on the other leg.

060 Reverse Lunge Knee Up

Standing with hands on hips, step back into a lunge with both legs bent. Push off the back leg, bringing the knee forward and up toward the chest. Swing the leg to land back again, with both legs bent. Repeat, stepping back on the other leg!

061 Barbell Reverse Lunge

Begin feet together, with the barbell behind your head, balanced on your shoulders, secured in both hands. Deeply bend into your Reverse Lunge, keeping the weight of your body on your front foot. Hold, breathe, and return to standing. Repeat, stepping back on the opposite leg.

062 Dumbbell Reverse Lunge

With core long and strong, begin with feet hip width apart, dumbbells in hands. Deeply, bend into your Reverse Lunge (#059), being sure not to swing your arms. Hold, breathe, and return to standing. Repeat, stepping back on the other leg.

063 Kettlebell Overhead Reverse Lunge

Take a kettlebell overhead in your right hand and open the left arm out to the side for balance. From standing step into a Reverse Lunge (#059) with the right foot. Keep both knees aligned over the ankles and your arms energized! Repeat on the left foot.

064 Plyo Touchdown Switch

This plyometric explosive move is one of the best high intensity ways to engage the hamstrings, calves, and lower back. If you are in need of a modification, try keeping a slight bend in both knees. Be sure to inhale and exhale deeply.

- Quickly move into your Lateral Lunge (#041), bending the right knee and tapping the right toe.
- Swing the arms up, into a jump, with your core and glutes engaged, and land to the left, tapping your left toe! Continue on alternate sides!

065 Switch Lunge with Jump

Take a wide open legged stance. Bend into a forward lunge with both legs bent, quickly jump up, switching legs in the air, and land on the opposite leg in a bent lunge position. Use the arms as needed!

066 Curtsy Lunge

Begin with feet together, arms out in front. Take your Lateral Lunge to the right, hold there, then cross the left leg behind your right, and hold there by engaging the fronts and backs of the thighs and squeezing your core! Repeat on the opposite side.

067 Jumping Lunge

Performing lunges and lower body workouts that incorporate jumping are a sure way to create better balance and coordination. The nervous system and spine are stabilized through this balance work too!

Let's Get Jumping!

Plyometric routines such as this Jumping Lunge are said to be some of the best exercises in the world! They are challenging, but if you can master them the results are astounding. Jump training can benefit you in many areas: aerobic endurance, dynamic explosive power, core strength, and cardiovascular health.

- Begin standing tall. Squeeze the abs in deeply and step into a forward lunge with both legs bent. Activate the legs and quickly jump up high, swinging your arms forward and up as you leap.
- Switch legs in the air, and land on the opposite leg in a bent lunge position.

068

Alternating Renegade Row

There is a reason that this movement calls itself the "Renegade" Row. A Renegade describes one who is unconventional and rebellious, and chooses to go against the grain. This exercise is indeed these things and so much more! Performing this move requires great concentration and the ability to focus on keeping a solid, unmoving core, coupled along with isolated, quick, dynamic rowing upper arm movements.

Correct form
Take care to keep your body in proper alignment while performing your Renegade Row. Arms should be under the shoulders.

Avoid
Don't let the weight of the body shift forward or backward. Keep your balance in a straight line with the kettlebells.

Annotation Key
Bold text indicates target muscles
Black text indicates other working muscles
* indicates deep muscles

deltoideus medialis

triceps brachii

deltoideus anterior

obliquus externus

transversus abdominis*

pectoralis minor *

pectoralis major

rectus abdominis

biceps brachii

- Holding the kettlebells securely in each hand, get into your best plank position. Make sure your abdominals are pulling strongly up into your back and that your legs are long and strong with the weight on the balls of the feet.

- With your body suspended, parallel to the floor, pull up your right hand, bringing the kettlebell in line with the side of your body. Be sure to keep your body still, isolating the arms only.

- Take turns pulling up and lowering each kettlebell, rowing right to left.

069

Single Leg Renegade Row

Start in the Renegade Row plank position with kettlebells under each hand. For this variation, lift the opposite leg and arm together for an added challenge! Remember to keep the center of your body good and still.

070

Single Arm T-Row

If you're in the mood to go for something a bit more challenging in your row, try this variation! The benefits will include a strong set of abdominals, super developed back and core muscles, and sleek shapely arms.

· Assume the flat Renegade Row plank position with kettlebells under each hand.
· Now, with your core deeply engaged and each arm energized, alternate turns, twisting and opening your chest to either side.
· Allow the arms to spin open to the sky each time.

071

Swiss Ball Weighted Row

Fitness experts recommend working dumbbells into your weekly workouts at least 3 times per week. Putting the chest and deltoids to work steadily will be sure to yield the best results!

Swiss Ball Stability

Performing this row variation on your Swiss ball, with the dumbbells, will greatly up your core strength. Incorporating weights into your row will target all of the muscles responsible for creating good posture in the upper back. This is also a great variation for someone who would like to work on developing more stability in the core and throughout the legs.

- Lie with your core centered over a Swiss ball, dumbbells in each hand.
- Your body should be in one line with your arms hanging down off the ball.
- Pull your abs up and in, bending your arms. Repeat!

072

Balance Ball Rows

Executing your workouts by incorporating an unstable surface, such as the balance ball, is a sure way to create better balance and coordination in the body. In this variation you are enhancing your core strength by balancing on one arm centered into your balance ball.

- Place your feet slightly apart while holding a strong plank position with one arm at the center of your balance ball.
- Take a dumbbell in your right hand and pull it into your chest. Engage your core and lower the dumbbell back down to start.
- Switch arms and continue, alternating sides.

073

Teapot Rows

Standing with feet hip width apart, walk your right foot up onto the box behind you. Take a kettlebell in your right hand and place the left hand on your hip. Bend your hips and tip the torso deeply forward, pulling the kettlebell into your chest. Alternate sides.

Figure 8

The Figure 8 move is great for those looking to stabilize their core while simultaneously developing a wider range of flexible upper body movement. You might also stretch your spine an inch or two (2.5 to 5 cm) once you master the maximum height of your Figure 8. If you are involved in an activity that requires you to twist or rotate the upper body side to side, such as tennis, golf, baseball, swimming, or shot put, this is an excellent move for you! You can challenge your range by adding a weighted Medicine ball, kettlebell, sandbag, or heavy disc.

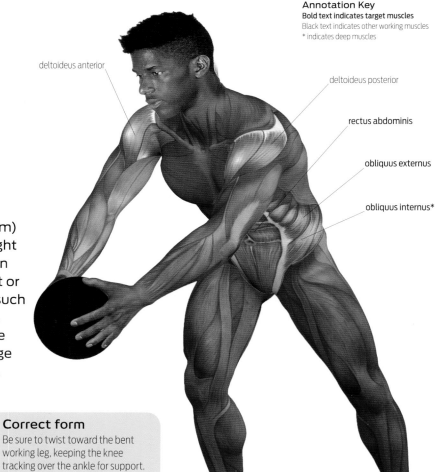

deltoideus anterior
deltoideus posterior
rectus abdominis
obliquus externus
obliquus internus*

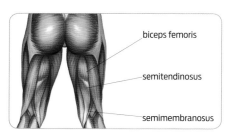

biceps femoris
semitendinosus
semimembranosus

Correct form
Be sure to twist toward the bent working leg, keeping the knee tracking over the ankle for support.

Avoid
Do not adjust the weight of your back foot until you have reached your maximum torso rotation.

- Stand tall with your feet under your shoulders. Hold a Medicine ball in your hands, at the base of your abdominals.
- Raise your arms and the ball on a diagonal, up toward your left shoulder, keeping your hips forward, but letting your right foot spin slightly up, lifting the heel. Look up toward the ball.
- Bring the ball and your arms back down into your center, making the shape of a figure 8, and repeat to the right.

075 Cable Woodchop

Standing with your feet shoulder width apart, take the cable in both hands out to the right and, in one smooth controlled motion, pull the cable across your body toward the left hip. Resist the cable and return to the starting position. Repeat on the other side.

076 Shoulder Height Woodchop

Take the cable as you would for the standard woodchop. This time, start higher up. Pull the cable straight across the body from shoulder to shoulder. Twist and rotate the upper body against your unmoving hips. Engage those abs!

077 Weighted Ball Woodchop

Moving through your woodchop will not only create deep stabilization of the hips and pelvis, but also fire up and stimulate all of your back and core muscle groups—inside and out. Swinging from side to side will also give you a deep stretch!

- Start with both feet wide, holding a weighted ball in your hands. Pull up the abs and engage the lower back and leg muscles.
- Twist your body to the right with the ball low, knees bent, and thrust, rotating the ball strongly to the right corner above and behind you, pivoting the legs.
- Change rotation of sides and repeat. For a challenge, add a heavier ball or disc.

078 Power Cross Chop

With wide legs, hold the Medicine ball out in front. Take a deep lunge to the left with both legs bent, swinging the ball over your left knee. Then stand, thrusting the ball right, up behind your shoulder, with straight legs. Change sides and repeat.

Annotation Key
Bold text indicates target muscles
Black text indicates other working muscles
* indicates deep muscles

079

Overhead Press

Overhead pressing has long been found in the world of workout. The ability to lift anything begins with having a functional and healthy spine and then radiates out to other supporting muscle groups. Specifically, lifting over the head enhances upper body parts such as the arms, chest, upper back, and shoulders. Having upper body strength allows other organs inside of the body to work better as well. Executing the Overhead Press with resistance straps or any weighted device will help in creating a stable shoulder girdle, long strong abs that lie flat against the spine, and, naturally, strength throughout the arms and across the chest.

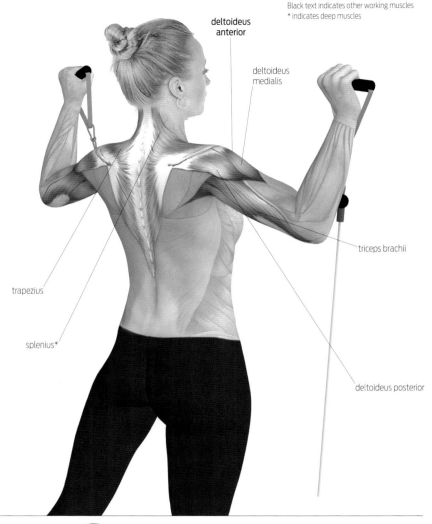

deltoideus anterior

deltoideus medialis

triceps brachii

trapezius

splenius*

deltoideus posterior

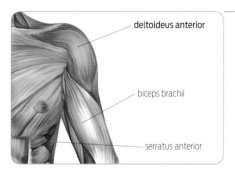

deltoideus anterior

biceps brachii

serratus anterior

Correct form
Try to keep your elbows, wrists, hands, and shoulders all in good alignment for your press.

Avoid
Do not push the chin out away from the back of the neck or clench in the shoulders.

- Start in a staggered stance with your upper arms at shoulder height, bent each at 90 degrees. If you are working with a resistance band, be sure it is secured safely under the middle of your front foot.
- Slowly straighten your arms up overhead by engaging your abs and your upper back strongly, working against the resistance of the band.
- Once your arms are completely straight, hold a moment, and then lower the arms back down.

080 Floor Press

Lie flat on the floor, holding a weighted Medicine ball to the chest. Exhale and brace the core while pressing the ball toward the ceiling. Inhale to lower.

081 Dumbbell Shoulder Press

Sitting down with abs pulling in, supporting the back, open the legs comfortably. Hold dumbbells in each hand, off the shoulder at right angles to the torso. Exhale, lifting the weights up at each side. Hold at the top, lower, and repeat.

082 Military Press

With dumbbells in each hand, stand up long against their weight, engaging the core and back muscles. Keeping the shoulders down, bend the elbows, bringing the weights to your shoulders, then press up overhead. Take care to maintain proper form!

083 4-Count Overhead Press

This press is done in 4 counts. Take a weight onto your left shoulder. On 1 raise the weight above your head, on 2 lower the weight to your right shoulder, on 3 return it overhead, on 4 lower to the left shoulder. Repeat!

084 Bulgarian Split Squat and Dumbbell Press

Get into a Bulgarian Split Squat stance with your arms at your sides, dumbbells in hands. As you squat, isolate the elbows to bend and then press up overhead. Keep your spine straight and shoulders down.

085 Bulgarian Split Squat with Overhead Press

With one foot elevated behind the other, find your Split Squat stance. As you bend into the squat, raise your arms overhead and hold. Both knees should be at 90-degree angles to the floor. Switch legs and repeat. Squeeze your glutes!

086 Inclined Bench Press

Adjust the bench so that the pad declines. Hook your feet under the bar at the higher end and lower yourself back. Press both dumbbells slowly overhead.

087 Swiss Ball Flat Dumbbell Press

Lie supported by the Swiss ball, with abs pulling in. Hold dumbbells in each hand, off the shoulder at right angles to the torso. Exhale, lifting the weights up toward the ceiling, hold at the top, lower, and repeat.

088 Swiss Ball Alternate Shoulder Dumbbell Press

Sit on the Swiss ball with abs and shoulders engaged. Arms should be at 45-degree angles from the shoulders. Alternate lifting and lowering each dumbbell, one at a time, overhead. Keep those shoulders loose and relaxed. Work the back!

089 Balance Ball Squat with Shoulder Press

Stand with both feet on a balance ball. Take a weight in each hand and raise overhead. Squeeze the core, glutes, and hamstrings to balance. Slowly descend into your squat, keeping a long spine while lowering the weights to chest height. Hold there, then stand, raising the weights again.

090 Medicine Ball Over the Shoulder Throw

Throwing over the shoulder is a great move for those looking to stabilize their core while also developing a wider range of rotation in the upper body. You will also stretch your spine and back as you increase the height of your throw.

- Start with both feet wide, holding a Medicine ball in your hands.
- Twist your body to the left with the ball just above hip height.
- Bend your knees, and thrust the hips to the right, rotating the ball strongly to the right corner behind you, pivoting the legs. Swap sides and repeat.

091 Balance Ball Arm Raise

Flip your balance ball so that the rounded side is facing up. Step to the center of your balance ball and hold your dumbbells long and loosely at your sides. Pull in your core and slowly raise your weights open to either side.

092 Balance Ball Side Plank with Lateral Shoulder Raise

Assume your side plank position, legs stacked, with one hand centered on the balance ball. Keeping the front of your body flat, raise your arm overhead up alongside your body. Maintain a long spine by stabilizing your core! Repeat on the other side.

093 Swiss Ball Rear Lateral Raise

Lie with your core centered over a Swiss ball, dumbbells in each hand. Your body should be in one line with your arms hanging down off the ball. Pull your abs up and in, isolate your elbows, and bring your arms out to your sides.

Russian Twist

Originating from the standard sit-up, the Russian Twist spices things up by adding the element of rotation from side to side in the torso. Being able to twist in this way, working against the pull of gravity, while keeping the lower extremities still and solid is indeed a great challenge, but will certainly reap huge benefits!

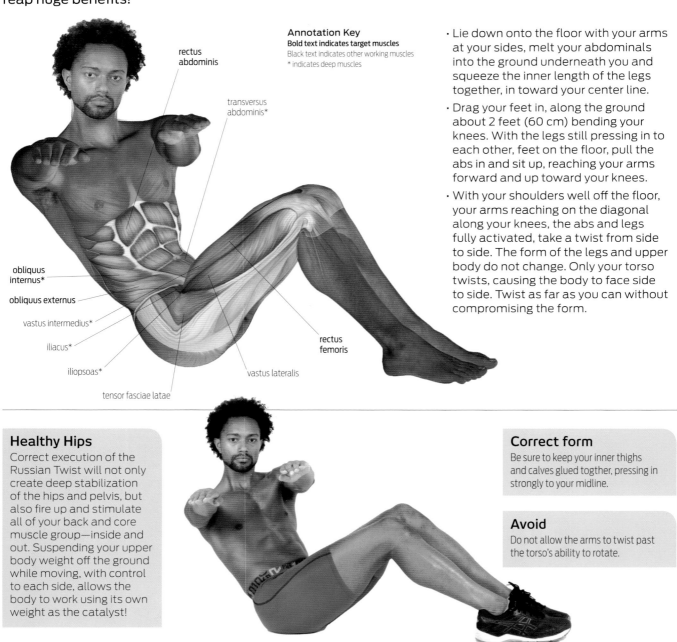

rectus abdominis

transversus abdominis*

obliquus internus*

obliquus externus

vastus intermedius*

iliacus*

iliopsoas*

tensor fasciae latae

vastus lateralis

rectus femoris

Annotation Key
Bold text indicates target muscles
Black text indicates other working muscles
* indicates deep muscles

- Lie down onto the floor with your arms at your sides, melt your abdominals into the ground underneath you and squeeze the inner length of the legs together, in toward your center line.

- Drag your feet in, along the ground about 2 feet (60 cm) bending your knees. With the legs still pressing in to each other, feet on the floor, pull the abs in and sit up, reaching your arms forward and up toward your knees.

- With your shoulders well off the floor, your arms reaching on the diagonal along your knees, the abs and legs fully activated, take a twist from side to side. The form of the legs and upper body do not change. Only your torso twists, causing the body to face side to side. Twist as far as you can without compromising the form.

Healthy Hips
Correct execution of the Russian Twist will not only create deep stabilization of the hips and pelvis, but also fire up and stimulate all of your back and core muscle group—inside and out. Suspending your upper body weight off the ground while moving, with control to each side, allows the body to work using its own weight as the catalyst!

Correct form
Be sure to keep your inner thighs and calves glued togther, pressing in strongly to your midline.

Avoid
Do not allow the arms to twist past the torso's ability to rotate.

095 Advanced Russian Twist

Assume the Russian Twist position (#094) and lift your feet off the floor, with the lower legs parallel to the floor. To do this, scoop the lower abdominals, pressing them deeper into the spine, and lengthen the back of the body, up and out of the head. Perform a Russian Twist while holding this position.

096 Swiss Ball Seated Russian Twist

Moving through your Russian Twists correctly requires the ability to lengthen the front of the hip, allowing the torso to rotate from side to side, while also stabilizing the core and lower extremities.

- Get into your Russian Twist position (#094) and take the Swiss ball into both hands.
- Twisting side to side, let the ball lightly graze across your knees each time you switch sides.
- Keeping your torso on an angle, will challenge the core!

097 Standing Russian Twist

Start with both feet wide, holding a Medicine ball in your hands. Twist your body to the right, knees slightly bent, and thrust to the left. Rotate the ball strongly each way, twisting and rotating the core, pivoting the legs.

098

Hip Twist

This variation gives you the opportunity to work the deep inner core muscles, which can be hard to reach sometimes. By keepng the legs elevated in the air and stabilizing from deep inside your core, you will strengthen both internal and external abdominal groups.

- In Russian Twist position, place both hands on the floor behind you.
- Extend legs off the floor into a V shape.
- Scoop the lower abdominals a lot and stabilize the hips, sway the legs to the right, and then left. Breathe!

Up and Out

Elevated leg twists are an excellent way to increase overall health in the body. Not only do they strengthen the core muscle groups, they are also great for stabilizing the lower back and aiding back pain. They are simple to do and require no props!

099

Spine Twist

Sit with legs long, feet together. With your torso tall, pulling up out of the hips, arms wide to the front, rotate the upper body to each side. Twist as far as you can while keeping the legs still.

100 Twisting Knee Raise

Stand with a long spine, legs apart, with your elbows bent and hands just above shoulder height. Twist your torso to the left and pick up your left knee, bringing the elbows to meet it. Switch sides, moving at an even pace.

101 Latissimus Dorsi Twist

Keep your heels rooted as you move through this rotating variation. The hips will need to hinge and move, bringing the entire shape of your torso to each side. Your legs should be long and supple, and your arms stretched overhead.

- Start with your legs squeezing in toward your center line.
- Interlace your fingers and flip your palms outward.
- Raise your arms overhead, and bend to the left from the hip.
- Roll your torso to the left, forward, and then to the right. It should be as if you are tracing a circle. Reverse directions and repeat.

102 Chair Twist

In a chair, inhale and exhale deeply a few times. Reach your right arm down, through your legs, to hold the lower part of the chair leg. Breathe deeply here. When you feel good and stretched, sit up and switch sides.

Barbell Deadlift

Taking on the deadlift, especially one with the barbell, will greatly up your core strength and core stability. Deadlifting a barbell targets all of the muscles responsible in creating good posture. You will be able to keep your back straighter throughout your various daily activities, too! If you are looking to do only one magical exercise that works all the body's muscles at once, this is the one to do. The deadlift works your lower and upper body simultaneously, including your back muscles. And, believe it or not, doing a few sets of Barbell Deadlifts will also increase your cardio ability!

deltoideus anterior
deltoideus medialis
deltoideus posterior
rectus abdominis
obliquus externus
gluteus maximus
brachioradialis
extensor digitorum
biceps brachii
brachialis
flexor digitorum*
transversus abdominis*
rectus femoris
vastus intermedius*
vastus medialis
sartorius
adductor longus
vastus lateralis

Correct form
The deadlift targets the lower back muscles and the hamstrings. Be sure to keep both parts of the body straight and long.

Avoid
Do not let the barbell swing or alter at all during this movement. Keep the weight in the center of your body.

- Stand up straight with your feet shoulder width apart, directly behind your barbell.

- Pull in your abs, bend your knees slightly, and bend forward from the hips.

- When your hands have reached the barbell, grip it tightly, engage your back muscles and core, and pull the barbell up along the front of your shins, all the way to your hips. Keep your arms straight the entire time. Lower the bar down again.

104 Barbell Power Clean

The Barbell Power Clean is a move that places the weight of your barbell directly in front of you. By lifting or snatching up the bar with a dynamic quick count, you work on developing core strength as well as stability in the lower back and legs.

- Start in a deeply bent squat position, holding on tightly to your barbell.
- In one move, pull the barbell up along the front of your body, high into your shoulders.
- Engage through the legs and core, and lower the bar back down again.

Tempo and Flow

It is important to note that speed is a dynamic component to consider when executing your upper body workouts. Moving in and out of repetitions with a slower tempo will develop long and strong muscles. Quickening your sets will build more stamina through cardio.

105 Barbell Power Clean and Jerk

Start in a deeply bent squat position, holding on tightly to your barbell. In one move, pull the barbell up along the front of your body, high into your shoulders. Press the bar up high, directly overhead. Engage through the legs and core, and lower the bar back down again.

106 Barbell Clean and Jerk Modification

The classic Barbell Clean and Jerk is one of the most effective exercises for building and strengthening the legs and back. If you are looking to define and chisel out these sections, mastering this move will do exactly that for you! Modify with weight as needed.

- Start in a deeply bent squat position, holding on tightly to your body bar.
- Engage the abs deeply and squeeze the backs of the legs.
- In one move, pull the bar up along the front of your body, high into your shoulders.
- Raise the bar overhead and engage the core before lowering.

107 Dumbbell Deadlift

Stand tall with your dumbbells at your sides. Bend forward at the hips generously. Straighten both legs and bring your weights to meet in front of you. Extend the back up to standing tall as you began. Repeat and keep your back flat as you move forward and back.

108 Single Arm Dumbbell Deadlift

Start standing with your core pulled in tightly, grasping a dumbbell in your right hand. Deeply bend the knees and hinge the hips back into your standard squat. Tilt to the right, pull the weight up alongside the body and open to the right hip. Switch sides and repeat.

109 Kettlebell Single Arm Deadlift

Start standing with your core pulled in tightly, grasping a kettlebell in your right hand. Deeply bend the knees and hinge the hips back into your standard squat. Extend the legs and pull the kettlebell up alongside the front of the body and open to the right shoulder. Repeat with the kettlebell in the left hand.

110 Single Straight Leg Kettlebell Deadlift

Holding the kettlebell with both hands, bend forward extending your left leg back behind you. Allow the kettlebell to pull your weight forward and down into the floor. Keep your abs engaged deeply. Swap legs and repeat.

111 Romanian Deadlift

The Romanian Deadlift is a similar move to the Power Clean and Jerk. In this variation you will take a deeper bend in the legs than your standard deadlift. With the weight of your barbell directly in front of you, bend the knees and work on snatching up the bar in one dynamic quick count.

- Start in a deeply bent squat position, holding on tightly to your barbell with an underhand grip.
- In one move, bend the knees, bringing the pelvis back toward your heels, and pull the barbell up as you rise into a standing position.
- Engage through the legs and core, and lower the bar back down again.

Get Low

If you are looking to tone the upper leg and glute muscles, deadlifts are an excellent way to do that. By isolating your hips and back into a bent position, you focus the work of the body into the legs. This produces sculpted and toned thighs, quads, hamstrings, and buttocks!

112 Stiff-Legged Barbell Deadlift

Stand up straight with your feet shoulder width apart, directly behind your barbell. Pull in your abs, and bend forward from the hips. When your hands have reached the barbell, grip it tightly, engage your back muscles and core, and pull the barbell up along the front of your shins, all the way to your hips. Keep your legs straight the entire time.

113 Hyperextension with Barbell

Start standing tall with the legs wide apart. Take your barbell and let it lie across the shoulders. Engage the biceps and upper back and pull the core up and in as you bend at the hips. Keep the back straight as you bend forward.

114 Good Mornings with Dumbbells

Start standing tall with the legs wide apart. Take your dumbbells and bring them to either side of your upper shoulders. Engage the biceps a lot and pull the core up and in as you bend at the hips. Keep the back straight as you bend forward.

115 Farmer's Walk

Stand tall holding your kettlebells in each hand. Step forward with the right leg, and then with the left. Alternate sides and repeat as if you were walking normally. Squeeze the core in tightly as you walk and keep the kettlebells at your sides.

116 Sandbag Flip

Stand up straight with a long spine. Open your legs wide and securely come into a deep squat, holding one end of the sandbag in front of you. Lengthen your spine with abdominals pulled up and tip the sandbag up and over, flipping it!

117

Battle Rope Side-to-Side Swings

If you are looking to have a full-body strengthening session and also up your cardio, battle ropes will give you this and more! Battle ropes, because of their wide range of movement, are able to give you a more dynamic workout, achieving and reaching far more angles than basic weights. Your core works a ton when using battle ropes, and your cardio kicks up to a high level.

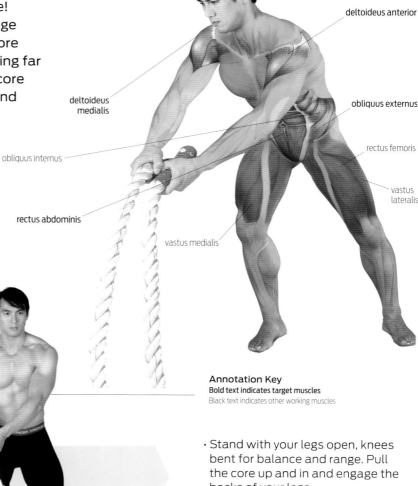

deltoideus anterior

deltoideus medialis

obliquus externus

obliquus internus

rectus femoris

rectus abdominis

vastus lateralis

vastus medialis

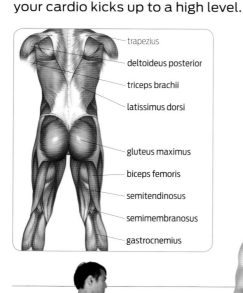

trapezius

deltoideus posterior

triceps brachii

latissimus dorsi

gluteus maximus

biceps femoris

semitendinosus

semimembranosus

gastrocnemius

Annotation Key
Bold text indicates target muscles
Black text indicates other working muscles

- Stand with your legs open, knees bent for balance and range. Pull the core up and in and engage the backs of your legs.
- Take the ropes in each hand and swing them to the left.
- Then, swing them to the right, rotating your upper torso against your hips and legs.

118 Battle Rope Alternating Waves

Stand with the feet shoulder width apart, holding on to the ropes firmly. Bend the knees slightly and begin with one arm tossing the rope up into the air, making a wave. Keep alternating arms, making waves, until you have achieved a consistent rhythm with the ropes.

119 Battle Rope Snakes

Stand with the legs securely shoulder width apart. Holding on to your battle ropes, begin by strongly swinging the ropes in toward each other, crossing the ropes, and creating snake shapes with the body of the rope.

120 Battle Rope External Rotation Spirals

Stand with the legs securely shoulder width apart. Holding on to your battle ropes, begin by strongly swinging the ropes out away from each other, then allowing the ropes to cross, and creating spirals that rotate out away from the body.

121 Battle Rope Claps

Stand with the legs securely shoulder width apart. Holding on to your battle ropes, begin by strongly swinging the ropes far out away from your center line. Bring the ropes back in to strike each other, making a clapping movement.

122 Battle Rope Crossover Slam

With battle ropes in hand, take a generous shoulder width stance. Lower into a squat position and, once at the bottom of your bend, explode the arms up together, flinging your ropes into the air, and then slam them to your outer left side. Take turns alternating sides.

123 Battle Rope Battle Jacks

For this challenging variation with the battle ropes, perform a standard jumping jack while holding the battle ropes in your hands. Jump the feet open wide while bringing the arms together overhead into a jumping jack.

124 Battle Rope Double Arm Wave

Take a shoulder width stance and begin with both arms tossing the ropes up into the air together, making two large waves. Keep thrusting the ropes up, making waves, until you have achieved a consistent rhythm with the ropes. As you move the ropes more, feel free to bend the knees as much as you need to in order to keep your balance and support the rope movement.

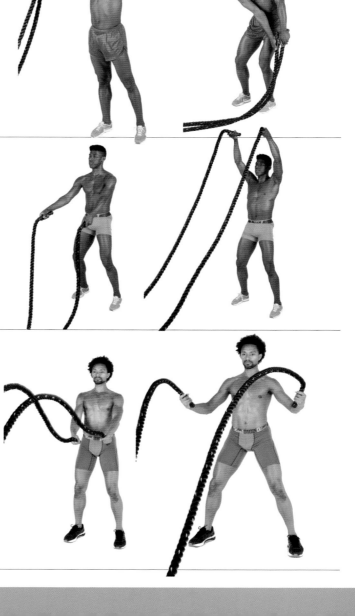

125 Battle Rope Double Arm Slam

Open the legs wide and take a bend in the knees, coming into an easy squat. With one big movement and a lot of force on the rope, fling the battle ropes up into the sky and slam them down strongly against the ground.

126 Battle Rope Double Arm Squat Wave

Keep your feet strongly and securely planted into the ground for this variation. Pay close attention to the size of your waves. Be sure to use a wide range of movement, creating a steady, large wave up and down.

A Good Rope Burn

The battle ropes are very commonly used today in workout routines. Creating alternating waves and jumps focuses the work throughout the body, deeply working the upper and lower extremities.

- With battle ropes in hand, lower into a squat.
- Remaining in squat position, toss the ropes up into the air together, making two large waves.
- Keep thrusting the ropes up, making waves, until you have achieved a consistent rhythm with the ropes.

127 Battle Rope Grappler Throws

Stand with your legs open, knees bent for balance and range. Take the ropes in each hand and swing them to the left, under the side of the body, with a rounded core. Then swing them to the right, rotating your upper torso side to side, while pivoting the feet.

Straight Kick

Straight Kicks, in which you swing and lift the leg out from the center of the body and then bring it back in, without moving any other part, are excellent for creating balance. Kicking in front, side, back, and adding shifts of the hips and pelvis also help with strengthening the core and enhancing stability in the spine and legs. Kicks can be found in a variety of workout routines and movement patterns throughout the world.

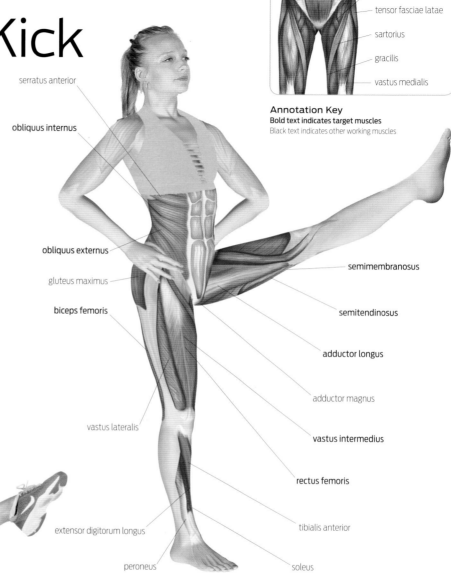

iliopsoas
pectineus
tensor fasciae latae
sartorius
gracilis
vastus medialis

Annotation Key
Bold text indicates target muscles
Black text indicates other working muscles

serratus anterior
obliquus internus
obliquus externus
gluteus maximus
biceps femoris
vastus lateralis
extensor digitorum longus
peroneus

semimembranosus
semitendinosus
adductor longus
adductor magnus
vastus intermedius
rectus femoris
tibialis anterior
soleus

Correct form
When you kick the leg out, take care to keep the hip of the moving leg down. Try not to hike the hip up in an unnatural way.

Avoid
Do not kick the leg with tons of force. The movement should be light and easy.

- Stand tall with your core engaged and the spine very long.
- Place your hands on your hips.
- Open the legs to shoulder width, and, in one movement, swing the left leg open to the front. Allow the weight of the leg to bring it back to starting, and then change sides.

129 Hand-to-Toe Lift

Stand tall and engage your abs deeply into the spine for optimal balance. Bring the weight of your body onto the balls of the feet. Bend the right knee, reach down with your right arm, grab the right toes, and extend the foot forward. Switch legs and repeat.

130 Kick with Toe Touch

Kicks with Toe Touch are excellent for stabilizing the core and stretching the hamstring and hips. They also help with strengthening the lower body and enhancing balance. If you are not yet able to reach your toe to touch it, aim to reach as far forward as you can.

- Stand tall with your legs open to shoulder width. Reach the right arm up.
- Engage your core and legs and swing the left leg out in front of you.
- Reach the right arm out in front of you to touch the left foot. Be sure to use a swinging motion in the legs and arms. Swap sides and repeat.

131 Kick with Arm Reach

Stand tall with your legs open to shoulder width. Engage your core and legs and swing the right leg out in front of you. Reach the left arm out very far in front of you and point the right foot. Be sure to keep your back straight. Switch sides and repeat.

132 Monster Walk

Stand tall with your spine long. Engage your core and legs and swing the right leg out in front of you. Reach the left arm for your right leg and flex the right foot. Be sure to use a swinging motion in the legs and arms. Walk forward, alternating sides.

133 Butt Kicks

Stand and squeeze the abs in very tightly. Bend into both knees and jump up quickly, extending your left leg and kicking your right foot back and up towards your hamstring. Move forward and alternate sides.

134 High Knees

Stand tall with your arms long at your sides. Engage the core and the backs of your legs and lift the right knee high into the chest. In one quick move, step the right leg down and bring the left leg up. Allow both legs to bend as you move through the variation.

135 High Knees March

Stand tall with your arms reaching straight out from the elbow at waist height. Engage the core and the backs of your legs and pull your right knee up to touch the right hand. Alternate and bring the left knee up to touch the left hand.

136 High Knees March with Arm Raise

Stand tall with your forearms reaching out long straight from the elbows in front of you, just below shoulder height. Engage the core and the backs of your legs and pull your right knee up high to touch the right hand. Alternate and bring the left knee up to touch the left hand.

137

Swiss Ball March

This Swiss Ball March variation is great for working on your coordination and agility. Holding the ball with your arms out in front of your shoulders, while alternating bringing in each knee to tap along the back of the ball, requires stability in the pelvis, upper back, and abdominals.

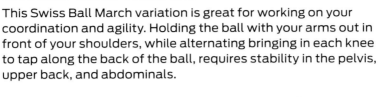

- Start with feet slightly apart and arms raised holding a Swiss ball.
- Reach the ball out very far in front of the body, and in one move bring the right knee up to touch the back of the ball, balancing on the left leg.
- Switch legs, and tap the left knee to the back of the ball. Continue to alternate legs.

138

Standing Knee Lift

Standing tall with your hands reaching out on the diagonal, step back into a lunge with both legs bent. Push off the back leg, bringing the knee forward and up into the chest. Swing the arms in opposition to the knee. Switch legs and repeat.

139

Abdominal Kick

Lie long on the floor with your spine straight. Bend your legs and bring them together at a 90-degree angle from your hips. Extend your left leg out and bring your right knee in, reaching both hands to hold the right knee. Alternate sides. Squeeze your abs in to support your core.

140
Side Kick

Static Side Kicks, in which you push the leg out from the midline and then bring it back in, without moving any other part, are excellent for stabilizing the sides of the body. They also help with strengthening the core and enhancing balance.

Annotation Key
Bold text indicates target muscles
Black text indicates other working muscles
* indicates deep muscles

trapezius

tensor fasciae latae

obliquus externus

sartorius

iliopsoas*

vastus intermedius*

vastus lateralis

rectus femoris

tibialis anterior

- Stand tall with your core engaged and the spine very long.
- Reach the arms long at your sides and open the legs to shoulder width.
- In one movement, swing the right leg open to the side and open the arms up wide to help keep you balanced. Flex the right foot.
- Allow the weight of the leg to bring it back to starting, and then change sides.

141 ## Knee Raise with Twist

Stand tall with your arms reaching long at your sides. Engage the core and the backs of your legs and bring your left knee up into the chest. Twist the upper torso against the left knee. Alternate and bring the right knee up. Allow the knees to swing gently from side to side.

142 # Knee Raise with Lateral Extension

This variation of the Side Kick challenges your balance, and strengthens your shoulders, triceps and forearms, as well as the leg muscles targeted in the Side Kick.

- Take a narrow width stance.
- From standing, open your arms wide to the side with dumbbells in hand.
- Bring the right knee up into the chest, and extend it out to the side. Take care to keep your arms out to your sides and energized! Switch legs and repeat.

143 ### Running in Place

Start with your biceps activated a lot and the elbows bent at the sides of the body. Pull in the core and squeeze the backs of the legs. Take a jog in place by lifting up your right calf and then the left. Try to kick your butt with the feet as you run.

144 Backpedaling

Start with your arms long at your sides. Pull in the core and squeeze the backs of the legs. Take a backward jog by lifting up your left calf and then the right. Put the emphasis on the backs of the hamstrings and try to kick your butt with each foot as you move.

145 Steam Engine

Stand tall with your hands at the base of your neck. Engage the core and bring your right knee up into the chest. Twist the upper torso against the right knee, touching the left elbow to the right inner knee. Switch legs and repeat.

146 Low Round Kick

Start facing forward in a wide open staggered stance with your right leg open behind the left. Turn your hips and feet towards your right. In one move, strongly thrust the hips to the front, balancing on the left foot, and kicking the right leg out.

147 Side Kick Reach

Stand tall with your core engaged and the spine very long. Reach the right arm up to the sky. In one movement, swing the right leg open to the side and bring your right arm to meet it. Flex the right foot. Bring the leg back down to stand and switch sides.

148 Switch Kick Punch

Stand tall with your legs open to shoulder width. Engage your core and legs and swing the right leg out in front toward your chest. Reach the left arm to your right toes on the diagonal. Point the right foot in the air and feel the stretch in the back of the legs. Alternate sides.

149 Martial Arts Kick

Kicks found in martial arts have been performed for hundreds of centuries. The execution of these kicks begins with balance and power from the legs and core. The kick moves should be performed in repetitive one-move swoops.

- Stand forward with the knees slightly bent, and bring your hands up to form fists at the chest.
- Pull the right knee in toward the body, engaging the core and hamstring deeply.
- Quickly kick the right leg out, turning the hips to face sideways, and flexing the foot. Switch sides and repeat.

150 Roundhouse Kick

Face forward in a staggered stance with your right leg open behind the left. In one move, strongly thrust the hips to the left side and kick your right leg out to the side toward the front, bringing the leg up very high. Repeat using the left leg.

151 Swiss Ball Side Kicks

Stand tall with your core engaged and the spine very long. Extend both arms up to the sky, holding your Swiss ball. Swing the right leg open to the side and bring your Swiss ball to meet it. Flex the right foot. Bring the leg back down to stand and switch sides.

152 Kneeling Side Kick

Kneel with the weight balanced on both knees. Place the left hand behind the head and the right hand down to support you. Shift your weight into the right side. Extend your left leg long out from the hip. Swing your left leg forward and then to the back. Switch sides and repeat.

153 Side Kick 1

As you move through your Side Kick variations you will see that they become increasingly more challenging, asking for you to up your core stability and deepen your abdominal strength. The key to Side Kicks is keeping your body in one long line as you allow the hip to isolate and move the leg freely and with control.

- Lie on your right side and bring your feet slightly forward from the line of your hips. Stack the legs on top of each other evenly.
- Let your right arm lie long under your head and place your left hand onto the floor in front of your chest for balance.
- Lift the left leg up about 1 foot (30 cm) from the right leg and pull the leg forward up to hip height.
- Push the leg back behind you and continue this front to back movement. Swap sides.

Pilates Power

Side Kicks have come to be associated with the movement guru Joseph Pilates. Pilates created a system of movements and exercises based on keeping the spine healthy. Ultimately, each movement in the Pilates technique aims to stabilize and strengthen the whole body from the core.

154 Bicycle Kick

This variation, the Bicycle Kick, gets its name from the action of the working leg. As you lie on your side, aim to bring the knee forward, under, around, and back, as if you were riding a bicycle. This bicycling movement is one of the more challenging isolations found in Side Kicks.

- Lie on your left side and bring your feet slightly forward from the line of your hips. Stack the legs on top of each other evenly.
- Prop your left arm up under your head and place your right hand onto the floor in front of your chest for balance.
- Lift the right leg up, bring it forward, and bend it into a right angle.
- Push the bent leg back behind you and extend it long to the back. Swap sides and repeat.

Hold Still

When executing Side Kicks, the side of your body that is flush with the floor should be still and unmoving the entire time. The working leg is isolated and moves on its own, supported by the pulling up and in of the core.

155 Side Kick 2

Lie on your right side and bring your feet slightly forward from the line of your hips. Stack the legs on top of each other evenly. Place both hands behind the head and prop up the right elbow for balance. Swing the left leg forward and then to the back. Swap sides and repeat.

156

Jumping

Jumping is a movement that we seem to do all the time as kids and, as we get older, we do less and less of it. This might be because jumping requires a lightness in the core. It requires energy and the ability to conjure up explosive power from the inside. You need to have a healthy, strong, and supple spine, and muscles that are agile throughout the body to support the movement of a jump. So, with these next few exercises we will get you jumping! Let's go!

- Start standing tall with energy shooting down into the feet and up out of the head.
- Bring your legs to shoulder width, and let the arms hang at your sides.
- Engage the core and bend both knees deeply.
- Pull the abdominals up and in sharply, push off the floor with your legs, and spring into the air.
- Come to land with both knees bent.

Annotation Key
Bold text indicates target muscles
Black text indicates other working muscles

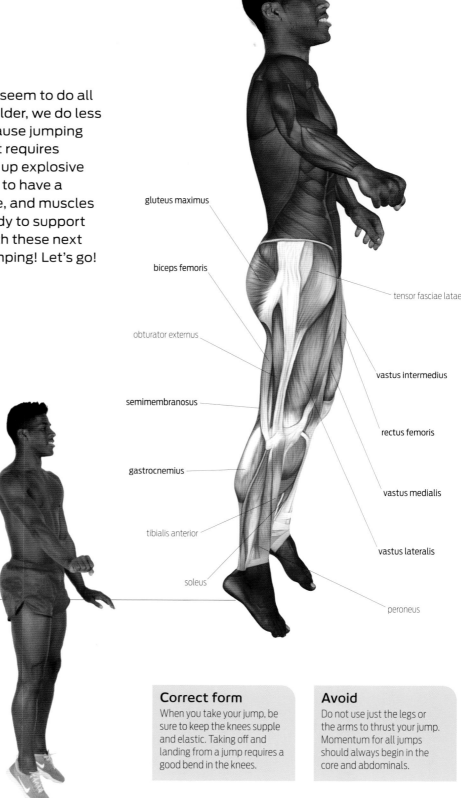

gluteus maximus

biceps femoris

tensor fasciae latae

obturator externus

vastus intermedius

semimembranosus

rectus femoris

gastrocnemius

vastus medialis

tibialis anterior

vastus lateralis

soleus

peroneus

Warm Up and Cool Down
To safely execute a jump variation be sure to have had a good stretch and warm up first. Stretching the hamstrings, calves, back, and ankles is very important. Your muscles should be nice and warm before attempting big jump variations. Warm up first, and also cool down when you are finishing.

Correct form
When you take your jump, be sure to keep the knees supple and elastic. Taking off and landing from a jump requires a good bend in the knees.

Avoid
Do not use just the legs or the arms to thrust your jump. Momentum for all jumps should always begin in the core and abdominals.

157 Star Jump

Crouch down into a standard squat position. Engage the abdominals and squeeze the hamstrings and quads. Spring open into a wide open air bound position, jumping up into the air, flinging your arms up and out to the sides and opening your legs wide.

158 Jumping Jacks

Jumping Jacks are a timeless exercise that yield great benefits when done correctly. In order to execute a perfect Jumping Jack, you must have a strong core and legs, explosive abdominal power, a healthy spine, good coordination, and supple muscles throughout the body. The Jumping Jack is done in two movements:
1. jump open and 2. jump together.

· Start standing with your feet together and your arms at your sides.

· Swing the arms up towards your ears and spring the legs open to the sides.

· Bring your arms together overhead, landing with your feet wide apart. Jump the feet back together and bring the arms down.

159 Jumping Jacks Clap

Start standing with your feet together and your arms at your sides. Swing the arms up toward your ears and spring the legs open to the sides. Bring your arms together overhead to clap, landing with your feet wide apart. Jump the feet back together and bring the arms down.

160 Scissor Stance Jacks

These Scissor Stance Jacks combine a good, rotational, side-to-side stretch of the arms and lower back against the legs, and then, in the final move, you come to jump straight up into the air bringing the legs to squeeze together. This well-balanced variation that incorporates all the muscles in the body.

- Start with the feet open in a wide shoulder-width stance. Bring your arms up and out to your sides.

- Reach the right hand to the left toes, bending forward at the hips with a rotation of the lower back.

- Then, swing and reach the left hand to the right toes.

- Stand up tall and jump high, bringing the feet and legs up and into your center line.

Jump Tips

Jumping strengthens the ankles and feet. Professional dancers, runners, and athletes across the board use jumping to improve the strength deep in the ankles and legs.

161 Straddle Leap

Start standing with your feet together and your arms at your sides. Bend very deeply, bringing your arms to bend up and into the chest. Explosively, swing the arms out to the sides and split the legs open to the sides. Reach the hands for your toes while in the air.

162 Stag Leap

Start standing with your feet together and your arms at your sides. Bend very deeply, bringing your arms up and into the chest. Explosively, swing the arms out to the sides and split the left leg bent to the front and the right leg bent to the back. Reach the hands overhead. Repeat with the right leg forward.

163 Tuck Jumps

Start standing with your feet together and your arms at your sides. Bend very deeply, swinging your arms out behind you. Explosively, swing the arms out in front and bring the legs up into the chest, tucking the knees up high.

164 Cheer Jump

Start standing with your feet together and your arms at your sides. Bend very deeply, bringing your arms up and into the chest. Explosively, swing the arms out to the sides and twist the hips to the right against the front of the chest. Bring the knees up and tuck them into the hamstrings. Repeat in the opposite direction.

165 Distance Leap

Start standing with your feet together and your arms at your sides. Bend very deeply, bringing your arms up and into the chest. Explosively, jump the legs out away from each other as if you are jumping over a hurdle. Reach the arms to assist with your jump. Continue, alternating legs.

166 Stadium Stair Jumps

Be very cautious not to miss your steps when jumping in this variation. Come to a surface like a stadium or staircase. Take a deep bend in the knees and use the arms to help thrust your jumps up one step at a time.

167 Depth Jumping

Start on top of a box. Take a squat, and quickly jump up high in the air, landing on the floor in front of your box with both knees bent. As soon as you land, extend the legs straight up, bend again, and jump back up onto the box. Use the arms as needed!

168 Up-Down

Start with the feet apart and under your hips. Swing the arms to the left, lifting the left knee, then to the right, lifting the right knee. Then, in one move, crouch down, hands to floor. Explode out into a plank. Quickly return to the crouched position. Last, fling the arms up to the sky, and stand tall with energy.

169 Lateral Bounding

Start with feet slightly apart and arms at your sides. In one move, jump up and to the side into a lateral moving lunge with both legs bent. Swing arms up, and then quickly jump up and to the other side. Keep changing sides.

170 Lateral Bunny Hops

Place your hands onto your hips and bring the legs in together, squeezing the inner thighs tightly in towards the center of the body. Engage the abdominals strongly and take a spring up into the air and to the left side. Quickly hop to the right side, alternating your jumps either way.

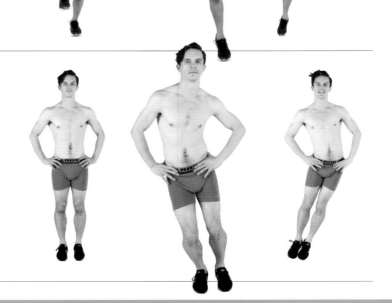

171 Side-to-Side Hop

Start with your feet together and arms at your sides. Place a body bar down onto the floor. Step to the left, hoping over the bar and swinging the arms. Angle your back over the bent knee with a long spine. Quickly, hop to the right and swing the arms again. Continue alternating sides.

172 Cone Jumps

In this variation you will find another workout incorporating plyometric moves. Plyometric refers to the idea of 'jump training'. Using the body's own weight and agility you move through routines that focus on enhancing speed and strength.

Add Some Weight

Try incorporating ankle weights into your jumping routines. It is a great way to boost aerobic activity while also strengthening the legs. You can use these weights every day while walking or jogging as well, increasing cardiovascular activity and blood flow through the body.

- Start upright, standing, with the feet close together.
- Open the legs to shoulder width and take a quick short bend on both legs.
- Explode up into the air, bringing both legs up and over the cone to the right side, moving about 1 foot (30 cm) from where you began.
- Use the arms to assist with your jumps as you move back and forth!

173 Slalom Jumps

Start standing with a straight spine and the feet shoulder width apart. Bend the knees into a standard squat. Reach the right arm outside of the right foot and bring the left hand to the right shoulder, change sides, and, finally, end in a deep bent-leg jump.

174 Side-to-Side Obstacle Springing

Start upright, standing. Open the legs to shoulder width and take a quick short bend on both legs. Spring up into the air, bringing one leg and then the other up and over to the side, moving about 1 foot (30 cm) from where you began. Use the arms to assist with your springing!

175 Box Jumps

Begin standing tall behind your box. Take a standard squat with both legs bent, quickly jump up high in the air, and land on top of the box with both knees bent. Extend the legs straight up, bend again, and jump back down. Use the arms as needed!

176 Box Jump with Ball

Begin standing behind your box holding a weighted ball in front of you. Take a standard squat with both legs bent, quickly jump up high in the air, and land on top of the box with both knees bent. Extend the legs straight up, bend again, and jump back down.

177 Straddle Box Jumps

Begin standing with your feet straddling a box. Take a standard squat with both legs bent, quickly jump up high in the air, and land on top of the box with both knees bent. Extend the legs straight up, bend again, and jump back down. Use the arms as needed!

178 Parkour Vault

Start standing with your feet together and your arms at your sides. Bend very deeply, bringing your arms up and into the chest. Explosively, swing the arms out in front of you to launch your body off of the vault. Bring the legs up into the chest, hurdling over the vault sideways.

179 Jump Cross

Performing the Jump Cross move requires great concentration and the ability to focus on keeping a solid core, coupled with isolated, quick, dynamic leg and upper arm movements. The benefits will include a strong set of abdominals, super developed back and core muscles, and sleek shapely arms.

- Begin standing tall. Bend the knees and come into a deep centered squat.
- Quickly jump up high, bringing the arms into your chest, hugging the elbows into your sides.
- Land center back in your squat and twist the body sharply to the left, striking your right arm out into a punch.
- Alternate sides and repeat!

180 Balance Ball Toe Taps

Start at one point alongside of your balance ball, rounded side up. Easily bend the knees and allow yourself to travel with a spring in your step, all the way around the circumference of the balance ball, tapping your feet on top of the ball as you go.

181 Ice Skater Hop to Balance Ball

Ice skaters spend a great deal of their time on the ice, pushing off of each foot to propel their bodies forward in space. In this variation you will learn how to push off the balance ball, utilizing it as an unstable base to help stabilize your knees, ankles, and core.

- Standing parallel alongside your balance ball, bring the hands into your chest.
- Bend into a deep squat and hop the left leg up onto the top of the balance ball.
- Hold here, and shift your weight onto your right leg, extend the left leg up into the air. Swap sides and repeat.

182 Balance Ball Box Jump

Begin standing tall behind your balance ball on the box. Take a standard squat with both legs bent, quickly jump up high in the air, and land on top of the balance ball with both knees bent. Extend the legs straight up, bend again, and jump back down. Use the arms as needed!

183 Jump to Balance Ball

Begin standing tall behind your balance ball. Take a standard squat with both legs bent, quickly jump up high in the air, and land on top of the balance ball with both knees bent. Extend the legs straight up, bend again, and jump back down. Use the arms as needed!

184 Straddle Balance Ball Variation

Begin standing with your feet straddling a balance ball. Take a standard squat with both legs bent, quickly jump up high in the air, and land on top of the balance ball with both knees bent. Extend the legs straight up, bend again, and jump back down. Use the arms as needed!

185 Skipping Rope

Skipping Rope is one of the ultimate ways to give your body a surge of cardiovascular activity while enhancing the ability to deliver explosive power at a high level over a prolonged amount of time. Performing the movement of Skipping Rope is also great for developing coordination and balance from the core.

- Start with the skipping rope securely in both hands, looped behind your body on the floor.
- Swing the rope over your head to the front of your body and engage the core and legs, taking a small hop over the rope as it passes under the feet to the back.
- Continue to swing the rope forward, jumping over it each time as it reaches the bottom of your feet.

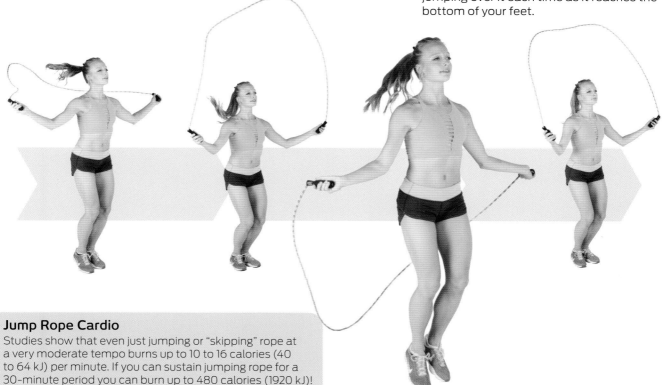

Jump Rope Cardio

Studies show that even just jumping or "skipping" rope at a very moderate tempo burns up to 10 to 16 calories (40 to 64 kJ) per minute. If you can sustain jumping rope for a 30-minute period you can burn up to 480 calories (1920 kJ)!

Burpee

The Burpee is said to be one of the best exercises in the world! It is not an easy move to perform, but if you can master it the results are astounding. Performing Burpees correctly can benefit you in many areas: aerobic endurance, dynamic explosive power, core strength, and cardiovascular health.

Correct form
You must strongly engage the abdominals and core throughout the Burpee movement. It is the only way to move through it smoothly!

Avoid
Do not let the lower back sink down while in your plank movement. Keep your alignment tight and secure.

Annotation Key
Bold text indicates target muscles
Black text indicates other working muscles
* indicates deep muscles

biceps brachii
deltoideus anterior
pectoralis minor*
pectoralis major
rectus abdominis
transversus abdominis*
vastus intermedius*
rectus femoris
vastus medialis

latissimus dorsi
obliquus externus
obliquus internus*
vastus lateralis
gastrocnemius
soleus

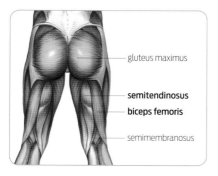

gluteus maximus
semitendinosus
biceps femoris
semimembranosus

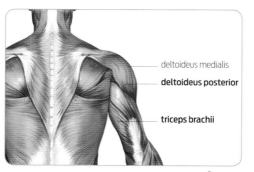

deltoideus medialis
deltoideus posterior
triceps brachii

- With feet apart and under your hips, raise the arms up to the sky.
- In one move crouch down, placing your hands to floor.
- Explode out into a plank position. Then quickly return to the crouched position.
- Last, fling your arms up to the air, leaping high with energy.

187 Medicine Ball Burpees

Medicine ball throws and tosses are a great way to enhance dynamic power, rotational flexibility and balance, as well as work on the nervous system's cross circuiting. In this variation of the Burpee, you will incorporate a Medicine ball, helping you stretch a bit more at the top of your explosive jump.

- Take a Medicine ball and firmly hold it in your hands.
- Squat down and put the ball on the ground in front of you.
- Engage your abs and jump the legs back into a plank Push-Up position, balancing on the ball and your feet.
- Jump the legs back into a squat, swing the arms up to the sky and jump.

188 Balance Ball Burpees

With feet apart and under your hips, raise the arms. In one move crouch down, hands to either side of the balance ball. Explode out into a plank. Quickly return to the crouched position, lifting the balance ball. Last, leap up into the air, pushing the balance ball overhead.

189 Side Burpee

With feet apart and under your hips, raise the arms up to the sky. In one move crouch down, placing your hands to floor. Explode out into a side plank position, extending your side body long. Then quickly return to the crouched position. Last, fling your arms up to the air, leaping high with energy. Repeat on the other side.

190 Renegade Row Burpee

Come into your best Push-Up position balanced on your kettlebells. Pull up your right hand and then your left hand, bringing the kettlebell in line with side of your body. Bring the legs into a crouched position, release the bells and jump up high.

191 Single-Leg Burpee

Performing Burpees correctly can benefit you in many areas: aerobic endurance, dynamic explosive power, core strength, and cardiovascular health. In this variation, you will focus the work on keeping your body balanced with just your two arms and one foot.

- With feet apart and under your hips, lift your left leg, and raise the arms up to the sky. In one move crouch down, hands on the floor.
- Explode out into a one-legged plank position.
- Then quickly return to the crouched position. Last, fling your arms up to the air, leaping high with energy. Alternate legs.

192 Tuck-Jump Burpee

With feet apart and under your hips, raise your arms to the sky. In one move crouch down, hands on the floor. Explode out into a plank position. Then quickly return to the crouched position. Last, fling your arms up to the air, leaping high and tucking the knees into the chest.

193 Single-Arm Burpee

With feet apart and under your hips, raise the arms to the sky. In one move crouch down, placing your right hand to the floor. Explode out into a plank position, balanced on one arm. Then quickly return to the crouched position. Last, fling your arms up to the air, leaping high with energy.

194 Burpee with Push-Up and Clap

With feet apart and under your hips, raise the arms to the sky. In one move crouch down, placing your hands to floor. Explode out into a plank position and do a Push-Up. Then quickly return to the crouched position. Last, clap your hands overhead up in the air, leaping high with energy.

195 Burpee with Pull-Up

Working all of the main muscles in the upper body region including the chest, back, shoulders, and both arms is the tried and true Pull-Up. This move is particularly challenging because, in performing it, you must be able to lift the entire weight of the body up just using the arms. Combine the Pull-Up with your Burpee for an exciting challenge!

Keep Your Form

It is very important to keep your abdominals pulled up and squeezing into your spine when performing your Burpees. Any sort of arch or hyperextension in the lower back could lead to strain and back pain.

- With feet apart and under your hips, raise the arms to the sky. In one move crouch down, placing your hands on the floor.
- Explode out into a plank position and do a Push-Up.
- Then quickly return to the crouched position.
- Stand tall and grasp your Pull-Up bar. Pull yourself into a Pull-Up.
- Repeat.

Power Punch

A Power Punch is a movement that derives straight from the power of the core. By shifting the trajectory of the hips and lower body from one angle to the next, you can send your upper extremities out into space with dynamic speed and strength. Developing a strong punch or strike of the arm will ultimately mean the development of strong core muscles, stemming deep from the pelvis, and even deeper into the muscles of the legs.

Annotation Key
Bold text indicates target muscles
Black text indicates other working muscles

trapezius

deltoideus anterior

deltoideus posterior

deltoideus medialis

rhomboideus

serratus anterior

erector spinae

rectus abdominis

latissimus dorsi

obliquus externus

obliquus internus

Correct form
Make sure when you deliver your power punch, or any other strike of the arm, that you keep one line from the elbow to the wrist.

Avoid
Do not break in the wrist, bending the joint too far forward or backward.

- Stand with the legs well staggered, the left foot in front of the right.
- Bring both hands into the chest, and make them into fists.
- Step forward with the right foot and strike the left arm out front.
- Then, in one move, punch forward with the right arm, bringing the left foot forward.

197 Cross Jab

In this variation, the Cross Jab is used as a punch of the arm that moves independently of the legs and hips. Working with your dumbbells in this punch sequence creates more work for the biceps and triceps. Keep your core and upper arms strong by engaging the abdominals and stabilizing the hips.

- Begin standing tall, with your dumbbells in each hand.
- Bend the knees and come into a deep centered position.
- Bring the weights into your chest and hug the elbows into your sides.
- Quickly, twist the body sharply to the left, striking your right arm out into a punch. Alternate sides and repeat!

198 Upper Cut

Stand with the legs well staggered and bent. Place the left foot in front of the right. Bring both hands into the chest, and make them into fists. Shift forward with the left hip and strike the right arm up into an uppercut. Alternate arms and foot stance.

199 Hand Clap Figure 8

With legs wide and toes turned out, squeeze your core and bend at the knees. Open the arms, engage your side abs, and reach both hands around the left thigh, clapping underneath. Stand, switch sides, and repeat!

200

Sit-Up

Correct form

When moving into your sit-up, curl through each part of your spine. This will ensure that you are really engaging each part of your abdominals.

Avoid

Do not pull on the neck with the hands to get your body off the floor. All of the work should be directly from the core.

The Sit-Up is a classic move that you are sure to find in just about all workout routines. Athletes and performers alike utilize Sit-Ups for their ability to stabilize and strengthen the upper body. The Sit-Up is a movement that works every inch of the core—from our multi-layered abdominals through to the backs of our bodies. Stabilizing the muscle groups that support our spine betters the total movement of our entire body, both upper and lower.

Annotation Key
Bold text indicates target muscles
Black text indicates other working muscles
* indicates deep muscles

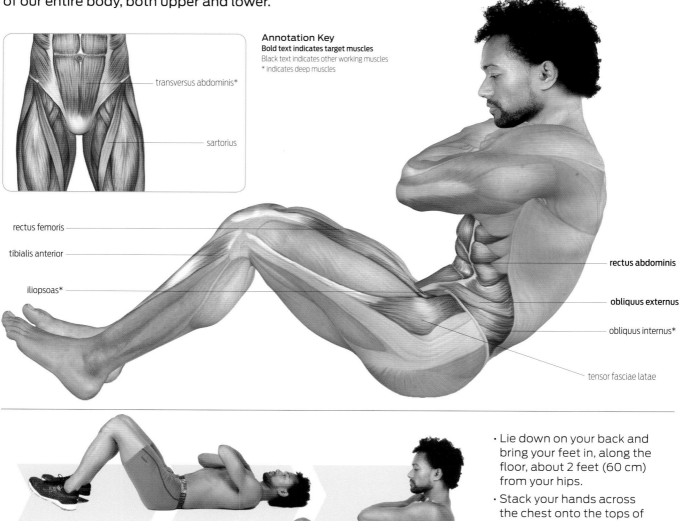

transversus abdominis*

sartorius

rectus femoris

tibialis anterior

iliopsoas*

rectus abdominis

obliquus externus

obliquus internus*

tensor fasciae latae

- Lie down on your back and bring your feet in, along the floor, about 2 feet (60 cm) from your hips.

- Stack your hands across the chest onto the tops of your shoulders.

- Engage your abs, tuck your chin into your chest, and curl your body up until your torso comes off the floor and is at a right angle to the floor.

201 Alternating Sit-Up

If you are looking to challenge the core a little deeper, and increase the stretch in your back and legs while performing your Sit-Up, try this rotated variation. This Sit-Up requires that you have a fair amount of flexibility in the obliques and hips.

- For this Sit-Up variation, begin lying down on your back with the hands behind the head and legs bent, slightly apart.
- Engage your core and sit up. Inhale and twist the body to the right, rotating against the base of your stable legs.
- Alternate sides and repeat.

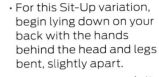

202 Turkish Get-Up

Lie straight along the floor and bend your right knee, bringing the right foot to the floor. Extend your right arm up, in line with your chest, and the left arm long along the floor. Slowly, keeping your right arm up, curl into a Sit-Up (#200), bringing the left foot onto the ground, and then stand. Repeat.

203 FR Sit-Up with Reach

Lay a foam roller flat on the ground, parallel to your spine. Position yourself to balance on the roller with your neck and spine supported and fully in contact with the prop. Keeping your legs bent and slightly open, straighten your arms above your head, and slowly roll yourself up into a Sit-Up on the roller.

204 Weighted Ball Sit-Up

Lie flat on your back with your legs bent. Hold a weighted ball in the center of your chest to begin. Squeeze your abs in and bring your torso all the way up into a Sit-Up (#200). Curl the body back down to lie flat, and repeat.

205 Balance Ball Sit-Up

Sit toward the edge of a balance ball with the flat side flush on the floor. Place your hands behind your head, and come into a standard Sit-Up (#200). The balance ball gives you an added element of balance and supports the lower back.

Basic Crunch

You can find the Basic Crunch mixed in alongside many other Sit-Up type workouts. Performing a crunch is, essentially, the beginning part of the full Sit-Up. With the crunch, you do not bring your full torso up into flexion. Instead, you squeeze the abs into the lower back, keeping the front and back sides of the body long and strong against the floor. This shortening of the abdominal wall deeply strengthens the many layers that make up our cores.

Correct form
Keep your lower back long on the floor and try not to arch your spine away from the ground under you.

Avoid
Avoid crunching the neck into your chest. You want to keep the neck long even if you cannot bring your body far up off the floor.

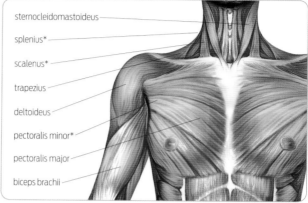

sternocleidomastoideus
splenius*
scalenus*
trapezius
deltoideus
pectoralis minor*
pectoralis major
biceps brachii

Annotation Key
Bold text indicates target muscles
Black text indicates other working muscles
* indicates deep muscles

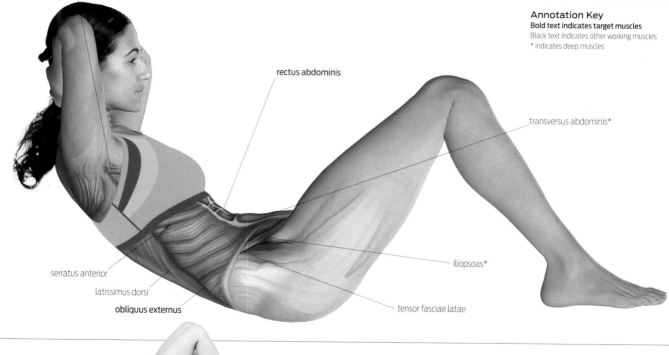

coracobrachialis

rectus abdominis

transversus abdominis*

serratus anterior

latissimus dorsi

obliquus externus

iliopsoas*

tensor fasciae latae

- Lie down on your back and bring your feet in, along the floor, about 2 feet (60 cm) from your hips.
- Stack your hands behind the lower part of your head.
- Engage your abs, tuck your chin into your chest, and curl your body up just until your upper back comes off the floor.

207 Crossover Crunch

Bend your legs and bring them together at a 90-degree angle from your hips. Come up into your crunch position and hold there. Extend your right leg out at 45 degrees and twist the upper body towards the left raised leg. Alternate sides and repeat.

208 Chair Ab Crunch

Sit on a sturdy chair and hold the sides of it firmly with each hand. Scoot your hips to the front of the chair. Engage your lower abdominals and core muscles and pull your knees up into your chest. Hold for a moment and lower the legs. Repeat.

209 Standing Knee Crunch

Incorporating some opposition into your crunch routine is a great way to keep your coordination sharp, as well as developing the cross-sections of muscles that run from the back of your body to the front. The abdominals and upper back muscles will become more stable when you bring this standing crunch variation into your workouts.

- Stand with your feet shoulder-width apart and bring your hands to the base of your neck.
- Explosively pull your right knee up into your chest and bend your torso to the right. Repeat on the other side.
- This move is great for overall coordination and control!

210 Swiss Ball Crunch

Performing these Swiss Ball Crunches is a great way to strengthen your overall core and, more specifically, your side abdominal walls and obliques. You can do them slowly to work on stability, or quicken your tempo to add a little bit of cardio into your crunch routine. Either way, it is a good way to warm up the core before any workout.

- Lie with your upper back supported by a Swiss ball. Allow the feet to be hip width apart down along the Swiss ball.
- Place your hands behind your head and push your heels into the floor.
- Engage the backs of the legs and squeeze the abs, curling up into your crunch.

211 Foam Roller Diagonal Crunch

Lie with your head and spine supported on the roller. With long legs, pull the abs in and come into your Sit-Up (#200). Simultaneously, lift the right leg, and bring the left arm up overhead. Diagonally cross your left arm to meet your right foot. Swap sides and repeat.

212 Balance Ball Crunch

Working with the balance ball in this crunch variation provides an unstable, soft surface for the lower back and core to stabilize on. Lie down on a balance ball with the flat side flush on the floor. Press into the balance ball and put your hands behind your head. Raise your torso up into a crunch.

213 Balance Ball Bicycle Crunch

Lie back on a balance ball. Bend your legs and bring them together at a 90-degree angle from your hips. Come up into your crunch position and hold there. Extend your right leg out and twist the upper body towards the left raised leg, bringing your left knee into the chest. Alternate sides and repeat.

214 Alternating Crunch

For this Sit-Up variation, begin lying down on your back with the hands behind the head and legs bent, slightly apart. Engage your core and take a crunch. Inhale and twist the body to the right, rotating against the base of your stable legs. Alternate sides and repeat.

215 Side Raised Legs Crunch

Begin lying on the right side of your body. Place your left hand behind your head and your right hand on your core. With the feet flexed, bend the knees into a 90-degree angle. Squeeze the abs in, lift the legs, and crunch into the left side of your abdominals. Lower, repeat, and alternate sides.

216 Balance Ball Oblique Crunches

Lie supine on a balance ball with your legs bent. Place your arms behind your ears, with your elbows out. Raise your head and shoulders up while contracting your trunk as you rotate your elbow toward the opposite knee. Lower, and repeat on the other side.

217 Oblique Bicycle Crunch

Bend your legs and bring them together at a 90-degree angle from your hips. Come up into your crunch position. Extend your right leg out and twist the upper body towards the left raised leg, bringing your left knee into the chest. Hold your torso in this position while extending and pulling in each leg in sequence. Repeat on the other side.

218 Reverse Crunch

Bring your legs together and your arms to your sides. Engage the core muscles and elevate the legs off the floor into a right angle. Press the arms into the floor and squeeze your legs into your chest for a reverse crunch.

219 Crunch with Medicine Ball Hold

From a laid out position, take a Medicine ball and hold it with both hands. Flex your feet and bring them up to the ceiling at a 90-degree angle from your hips. Keep your legs there, tuck your chin, squeeze your abs, and come into a Sit-Up reaching the ball up along your shins.

220 Diagonal Crunch

Begin sitting up with a strong core. Open your legs so that they are wider than shoulder width. With a Medicine ball, roll the body down to lie flat on the floor, leaning slightly to the right. In one move, lift the ball overhead and come into a dynamic Sit-Up. Roll down to the left. Alternate sides and repeat.

221 L-Sit

Sit with your legs straight in front of you, your hands placed next to your hips, palms down. Press strongly into the floor and push yourself up so that your butt and legs rise from the floor. Hold for as long as you can.

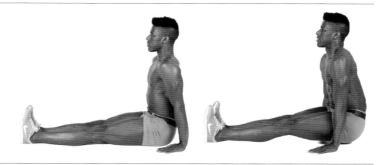

222 Trampoline Ab Crunch

Bend your legs and bring them together off of the trampoline at a 90-degree angle from your hips. Place the hands behind your head, engage the abdominals, and come up into your crunch position. Hold at the top of your crunch.

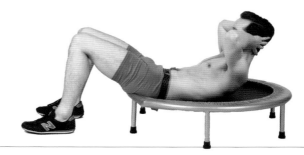

223 Trampoline Alternating Diagonal Ab Crunch

Incorporating a trampoline into your Sit-Up routines is a great way to work on enhancing your body's natural sense of balance and stabilization. The trampoline acts as an unstable base, giving you the opportunity to really deepen the work of the core muscle groups.

- Bend your legs and bring them together at a 90-degree angle from your hips.
- Come up into your crunch position and hold there.
- Extend your right leg out and twist the upper body towards the left raised leg, bringing your left knee into the chest. Continue, alternating sides.

224 Dumbbell Side Crunch

Stand with your feet wide open. Raise your right arm up into the air holding a dumbbell. Explosively pull your right knee up toward your shoulder, while bringing your right elbow down to meet it. Alternate sides! This move is great for overall coordination and balance control!

225 Swiss Ball Bridge Curl-Up

Lie with your back long against the floor. Engage the abs so that they are pulled deeply into the lower back, and bring your calves onto the Swiss ball. Squeeze your inner thighs together, press into your arms along the sides of the body and come into a crunch.

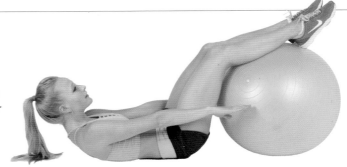

226 McGill Curl-Up

Begin with the body flat on the floor. Place your hands behind your lower back, and bend your left leg in. Engage your lower abdominals deeply and come up into a crunch. Keep the neck long and the eyes gazing out beyond your bent knee. Swap legs and repeat.

227 Turtle Shell

Start lying flat on your back with your legs long and extended open wide. Squeeze your abs in and bring the right leg straight up in line with the hip, reaching the arms open wide to the sides. Curl the torso and shoulders up off the floor towards the raised leg. Swap legs and repeat.

228 45-Degree Twist

Come to balance with the legs bent together, hovering off the floor. With your torso long, pulling up out of the hips, arms reaching to the front with your Medicine ball, rotate the upper body to the each side. Twist as far as you can while keeping the legs still.

229 Rocky Solo

Sit with legs long, feet apart. With your torso tall, pull up out of the hips, hands holding a Medicine ball. Take a rotation to each side. Twisting as far as you can while keeping the legs still, place the ball onto the floor.

230 Balance Ball Ab Twist

Take a plank, balancing on the balance ball, with your arms long out in front of you. Take a twist from side to side, bringing each knee in and across the chest. Keep your torso on an angle, challenging the core!

231 Balance Ball Ab Roll-Backs

Begin sitting up on the balance ball. Ground your tailbone, down into the middle of the balance ball, for balance. Holding a Medicine ball, extend your arms forward. Slowly lower the body back until your shoulders reach the balance ball. Sit back up again.

232 Foam Roller Side to Side

One of the most challenging ways to enhance your twist is by performing it on a foam roller. The cylinder shape of the roller asks you to find your balance while maintaining constant contact between the roller and your spine.

- Lay a foam roller flat on the ground, parallel to your spine.
- Position yourself to balance on the roller with your neck and spine supported and fully in contact with the prop.
- Keeping your legs bent and slightly open, straighten your arms above your chest while holding a Medicine ball.
- Slowly rotate your arms from side to side.

233 Foam Roller Twist

Keeping your legs bent and slightly open, sit up straight on a foam roller. Bring your arms into the chest and hold your weighted ball tightly. Twist the Medicine ball from right to left, rotating the torso and engaging the core and legs.

Swiss Ball Triceps Extension

Isolating the work of the arms while incorporating dumbbells, barbells, or any kind of weight will help define the muscles of the back, arms, and chest. Small movements overhead also help in stabilizing both large and small muscles throughout the upper body and core.

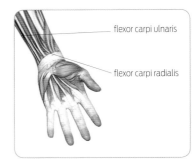

flexor carpi ulnaris

flexor carpi radialis

Annotation Key
Bold text indicates target muscles
Black text indicates other working muscles
* indicates deep muscles

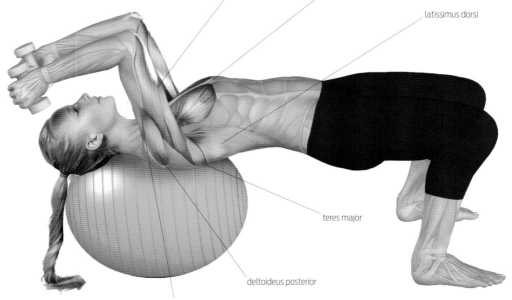

triceps brachii

pectoralis major

latissimus dorsi

teres major

deltoideus posterior

deltoideus anterior

Correct form
Be sure to isolate your elbow movement. Only bend and straighten from the joint, and not the shoulder.

Avoid
Do not let the upper spine arch up away from the Swiss ball. Keep the muscles of the upper back weighted and into the ball.

- Lie with your core deeply engaged, the Swiss ball supporting your upper back.
- Bring your feet open to shoulder width.
- Raise the dumbbells in your hands out from the chest so that your forearms are parallel to your face.
- Slowly, extend the dumbbells overhead, bending your arms and engaging the back.

235 Swiss Ball Pullover

Lie with your core deeply engaged, the Swiss ball supporting your upper back. Bring your feet open to shoulder width. Raise the dumbbells in your hands out from the chest so that your forearms are parallel to your face. Slowly extend the dumbbells up overhead, keeping your arms straight and engaging the back.

236 Swiss Ball Single-Arm Triceps Kickback

Triceps are the pair of muscles that run from the elbow joint to the shoulder on the back of the arm. The back parts of our muscle groups can, at times, be challenging to reach. In this exercise, you bring the focus on shaping and strengthening the tricep while stabilizing the core by incorporating a Swiss ball.

- Place your left arm firmly down into a Swiss ball so that it is supporting the weight of your torso.
- Come into a kneel and bend forward from the hips, with the balls of the feet on the floor.
- Take a dumbbell into your right hand and bring it alongside your Swiss ball.
- Squeeze the core and isolate your right elbow and bend the arm into a right angle. Extend the right arm straight to the back and engage the tricep. Alternate sides.

Totally Engaged

It is important to remember, whenever you are working the upper body muscles with hand weights or cables, to keep the larger muscle groups engaged and not tense, while working the smaller muscles in that area. The neck and shoulder muscles are intricate and can be easily be harmed if you use incorrect alignment or too much force.

237 One Arm Cable Extension

Begin standing in front of your cable. Grasp the cable handles, pull in your abs, lengthen the spine out of the top of the head, and pull down on the handles. With resistance, raise your ropes up again.

238 Foam Roller Triceps Roll-Out

Start on your knees with the foam roller on the floor. Place your hands on the roller with arms extended. Using your abs, roll the foam roller out straight from your hips, bringing your lower arms to touch the roller.

239 Swiss Ball Fly

Start lying with your upper back supported on your Swiss ball. Engage your core to support the lower back. With a dumbbell in each hand, open the arms to your sides, keeping a slight bend on each elbow. Then raise and extend the arms out in front of your chest.

240 Swiss Ball Weighted Reverse Fly

Lie with a Swiss ball under your upper torso. Extend your legs long and balance on the balls of your feet. Squeeze your abs deeply to help you balance and open your arms to the sides with dumbbells in hand. Hold open, then lower.

241 Swiss Ball Overhead Dumbbell Extensions

Start sitting up tall on your Swiss ball. Engage your core in to support your upper and lower back. Take a dumbbell in each hand, and press them up overhead. Isolate the elbows and bend the weights behind the shoulders. Straighten and repeat.

242 Swiss Ball Preacher Curls

Start sitting on a Swiss ball with your core engaged strongly into your back. Take a barbell and hold it hanging out in front of your knees. Isolate the elbows, and bring the bar into your chest. Keep the elbows tight into your sides. Lower and repeat.

243 Swiss Ball Dumbbell Curls

The standard curl is featured in all upper body workouts. Incorporating dumbbells, weights, or resistance bands while performing curls will help chisel out beautiful chest, shoulder, and arm muscles. Combining curls with exercises that focus on the core will help to strengthen muscles in the back, shoulders, and biceps.

Curl Deeper

Performing your weighted curls on a Swiss ball is a great way to take advantage of an unstable base underneath you. The Swiss ball provides a surface that requires you to squeeze your core in deeply and engage your back muscles, in order to keep your balance.

- Sitting tall on your Swiss ball, with the chest open, feet wide apart, hold the dumbbells with each hand in below the hips.
- Curl the weights up toward your shoulders, isolating the elbows at your sides.
- Once the dumbbells have reached level with your shoulders, lower them and repeat.

244 Swiss Ball Weighted Ab Curl

Lie with your lower back supported by the Swiss ball. With your weighted ball overhead, to start, slowly bring your arms over the chest and then up onto the diagonal. Keep your torso on an angle, challenging the core!

T-Stabilization

By utilizing your side T-Stabilization in this plank variation, you enhance the ability to stabilize not only the core, but also the shoulders and rotator cuffs. Executing this movement targets the transverse abs, obliques, and all the many layers of abdominals we have running along the upper body. Change your focus from side to side, keeping the body in one strong and long shape throughout the exercise.

Avoid
Do not move your arms too much in this exercise. Keep the movement isolated, spinning open from side to side.

Correct form
Be sure when working your side stabilization that the core muscles are all activated and helping engage the arms.

Annotation Key
Bold text indicates target muscles
Black text indicates other working muscles

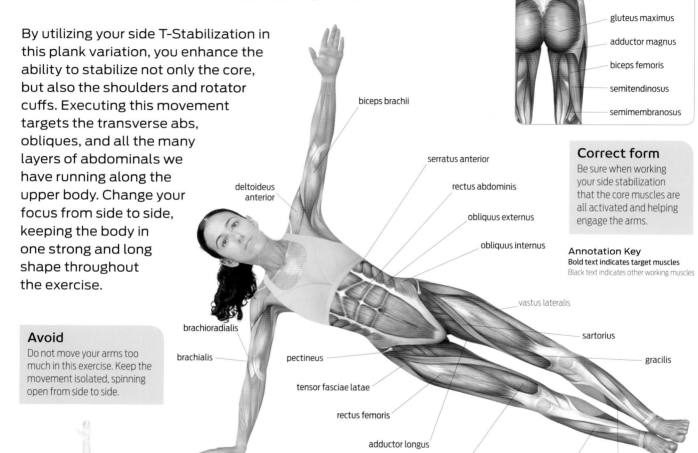

deltoideus posterior
triceps brachii
latissimus dorsi
gluteus medius
gluteus maximus
adductor magnus
biceps femoris
semitendinosus
semimembranosus

biceps brachii
serratus anterior
rectus abdominis
obliquus externus
obliquus internus
deltoideus anterior
vastus lateralis
brachioradialis
sartorius
brachialis
gracilis
pectineus
tensor fasciae latae
rectus femoris
adductor longus
vastus medialis
tibialis anterior
extensor digitorum longus

- Start in your standard plank with both palms flush with the floor under you.
- Shift the weight of your feet onto the side of one foot, stacking your feet on top of each other.
- Spin your upper body open and balance on one hand, stabilizing your side body and core. Hold here.
- Come back into your centered plank and spin open to the other side.

246 T-Stabilization with Dumbbells

Fitness experts recommend working dumbbells into your weekly workouts at least 3 times per week. Coupling your T-Stabilization with weights puts the chest and deltoids to work, while working the core and legs.

- Start in your standard plank balanced on top of your dumbbells.
- Shift the weight of your feet onto the sides.
- Spin your upper body open and balance on one weight, stabilizing your side body and core. Hold here.
- Come back into your centered plank and spin open to the other side.

247 Suspended T-Stabilization

Start in your standard plank with both palms flush with the floor under you. Walk your feet into a set of suspension straps. Spin your upper body open and balance on one hand, stabilizing your side body and core.

248

Kneeling Forearm T-Stabilization

Start with your left forearm down on the floor. Come into your side plank. Bend the left leg under your body, and stretch the right arm up to the ceiling. Squeeze the abs in, keep the body to the front and balance there. Repeat on the other side.

249

T-Stabilization with Leg Raise

Start with your left forearm down on the floor. Come into your side plank by extending the legs long, stacking the feet on top of each other. Stretch the right arm up to the ceiling, squeeze the abs in, keep the body to the front and extend the right leg up. Repeat on the other side.

250

Plank with Rotation

Push up into a center plank with your body supported by both of your arms. Engage the legs and core and twist your lower body from the hips down to the left. Bend your knees, and bend the arms. Take turns alternating, twisting to each side.

251 T-Stablization Twist

Incorporating some opposition into your T-Stabilization and side crunch routine is a great way to keep your nervous system sharp, as well as develop the cross-sections of muscles that run from the back of your body to the front. The abdominals and upper back muscles will become more stable when you bring this crossover twist variation into your workouts.

- Start in your standard plank with both palms flush with the floor under you.
- Shift the weight of your feet onto the sides.
- Spin your upper body open and balance on one hand, stabilizing your side body and core.
- Take the extended arm and reach it under your torso, curving the body into a rotated shape. Switch sides and repeat.

The Perfect Plank

Planks are one of the most simple moves to do. They are excellent for building up those deep inner core muscles that provide stability for your lower back. Planks are also excellent for improving posture, balance, and reducing back pain.

252 T-Stabilization with Reach Under

Start with your left forearm down on the floor. Come into your side plank by extending the legs long, stacking the feet on top of each other. Stretch the right arm up to the ceiling, squeeze the abs in, keep the body to the front and curve the right arm under your left side. Switch sides and repeat.

Basic Mountain Climber

Mountain Climbers are coined so because of the challenge they pose in alternating the legs up and into the chest while keeping the core and leg muscles fully engaged and flat to the floor, working against gravity as if you were climbing. This move will create stability in the core and the arms, and deliver the ability to produce explosive movement.

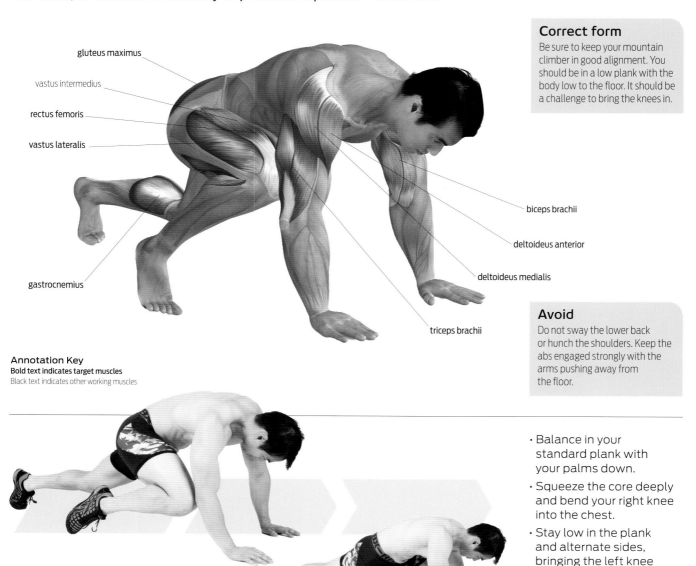

gluteus maximus

vastus intermedius

rectus femoris

vastus lateralis

gastrocnemius

biceps brachii

deltoideus anterior

deltoideus medialis

triceps brachii

Correct form
Be sure to keep your mountain climber in good alignment. You should be in a low plank with the body low to the floor. It should be a challenge to bring the knees in.

Avoid
Do not sway the lower back or hunch the shoulders. Keep the abs engaged strongly with the arms pushing away from the floor.

Annotation Key
Bold text indicates target muscles
Black text indicates other working muscles

- Balance in your standard plank with your palms down.
- Squeeze the core deeply and bend your right knee into the chest.
- Stay low in the plank and alternate sides, bringing the left knee into the chest.

254 Suspended Mountain Climber

Working with suspended cable straps gives you the opportunity to enhance your exercise by including the element of gravity. Pulling or pushing down or up against an added amount of gravity creates more strength, balance, and stability in the muscle.

- With your feet suspended off the ground in your straps, hold the arms very long and strong at a 90-degree angle to your body.
- Keep your upper body straight and engage the upper abs.
- Pull your right leg into your chest, and then the left.
- Hold with your legs together after each set for an added challenge!

255 Balance Ball Mountain Climber

Balance in your standard plank with your palms down at the center of your balance ball. Squeeze the core deeply and bend your left knee into the chest. Stay low in the plank and alternate sides, bringing the right knee into the chest.

256 Medicine Ball Climbers

Balance in your standard plank with your palms down over the top of a Medicine ball. Squeeze the core deeply and bend your right knee into the chest. Stay low in the plank and alternate sides, bringing the left knee into the chest.

257 Cross Body Mountain Climber

Come into an upright straight-armed plank. Engage the core deeply and bend your left knee into the center of the chest, between the arms. Move the leg across the body and then back. Stay low in the plank and alternate sides. Pick up the tempo bringing the knees in quickly for added cardio.

258 Spider Mountain Climber

Balance in your standard plank with your palms down. Squeeze the core deeply and bend your left knee out beside your right leg. Bend your arms as you alternate legs. Stay low in the plank as you change sides.

259 Sliding Mountain Climber

Come into your standard plank. Squeeze the core deeply and bend your right knee into the center of the chest, sliding the foot along the floor. Stay low in the plank and alternate sides, sliding the left knee into the body to the left shoulder.

260 Fire Hydrant Mountain Climber

Come into a plank with your arms supported on the floor. Push down with your hands and alternate bringing your left knee up to your left elbow, then your right knee to your right elbow. Keep the arms straight and the core engaged.

261 Swiss Ball Mountain Climber

Balance in your standard plank with your palms down at the center of your Swiss ball. Squeeze the core deeply and bend your left knee out beside your right leg. Stay low in the plank and alternate sides, bending the right knee out beside the left leg.

262 Foam Roller Cross Climbers

Take a plank, balancing on the foam roller, with your arms long out in front of you. Take a twist from side to side, bringing each knee in and across the chest. Keep your torso on an angle, challenging the core!

263 Bear Crawl

Bring your body into a plank. Bend your arms and bring your hands under your shoulders and squeeze the legs. Engage the abs strongly, and begin crawling your body forward, moving your hands and knees while keeping the core curved and engaged.

264 Crab Crawl

Crab Crawls are challenging because they require you to engage all muscle groups in the back and front body in order to stay in balance while moving forward. They are great for stabilizing the shoulder and upper back, as well as the pelvis and hip rotators.

- Start sitting on the floor with your legs extended out in front of you.
- Place your hands behind your hips and push into the floor.
- Elevate your hips up off the floor by squeezing your abs deeply.
- Bend your legs, and take a walk around in your Crab Crawl shape.

265 Alligator Crawl

Lie face down along the floor. Bend your arms and bring your hands under your shoulders and push up into your plank. Squeeze the legs, engage the abs strongly, and begin crawling your body forward, moving your hands and knees while staying close to the floor.

Push-Up

Correct form
Be sure to keep the body in one straight line the entire time you perform your Push-Up! This challenging stance requires you to work your abdominals while simultaneously engaging the arms isometrically!

Avoid
Pay special attention to your lower back region and your tailbone. Maintain a neutral pelvis—one that is neither arching back behind you or tucking forward.

The simple and beautiful standard Push-Up is one of the very best movements to master. Whether you are looking to have chiseled sleek arms or tight strong abs, doing Push-Ups will give you both, and so much more. From an upright plank position, the Push-Up requires you to lower slowly into and away from gravity, all while isolating the bed of your elbows.

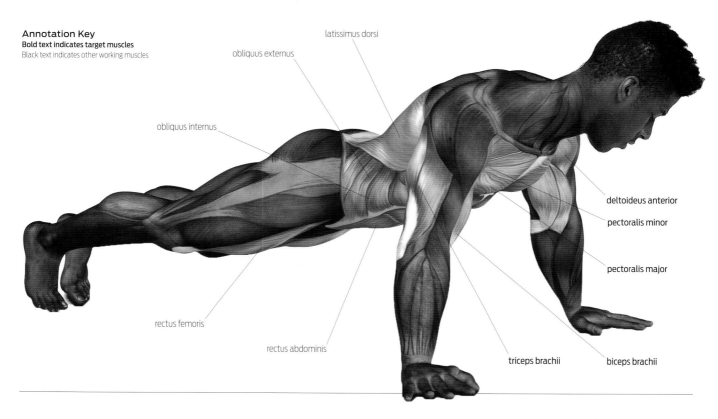

Annotation Key
Bold text indicates target muscles
Black text indicates other working muscles

latissimus dorsi

obliquus externus

obliquus internus

deltoideus anterior

pectoralis minor

pectoralis major

rectus femoris

rectus abdominis

triceps brachii

biceps brachii

- Start with your body long and parallel to the floor, balanced on your hands and balls of the feet.

- Keeping the sensation of floating by pulling up the abs tightly in toward the back, slowly isolate the elbows, bending at the joints, bringing your chest to meet the ground below you.

267 Push-Up with Clap

Lower into your Push-Up and, in one explosive count, push off the floor with both hands, and clap the hands together quickly, in front of the chest. Open the hands and land again in your low Push-Up.

268 Plyo Kettle Ball Push-Up

This Push-Up variation maximizes force with its quick intervals between moves. Start in your Push-Up form with the right hand over the kettlebell. Bend the arms into a Push-Up, quickly straighten the arms, and switch the kettlebell into the opposite hand. Repeat!

- Set a kettlebell down under your right shoulder and perch on top of it with your right hand securely balanced on the handle.
- Bring your left arm wide open into a Push-Up stance.
- Keeping your weight forward over your arms, slowly lower into your Push-Up, just until your pecs are in line with the handle.
- Bring your left hand to the kettlebell, switch hands, and take a Push-Up with your right hand open to the floor.

269 Dynamic Box Push-Up

Bend the arms into a Push-Up on either side of a box. Quickly spring off the floor, bringing both hands together in the air, landing in a Push-Up on top of the box. Extend the arms, lower into a Push-Up, spring off the box, opening the arms to land in your Push-Up straddling the box, as you began.

270 Single Arm Push-Up

Start in your straight-armed Push-Up position (#266). Place your left hand behind your back. Slowly, while keeping the left shoulder in line with the right, perform your Push-Up. Switch arms and repeat.

271 Single Arm, Single Leg Push-Up

With the weight evenly placed on both hands and the balls of the feet in your Push-Up stance (#266), raise the left arm off the floor, straight out in front of you. Then raise the right leg, straight out behind you. With balance, lower into your Push-Up. Swap sides and repeat.

272 Decline Push-Up

Come to your hands and knees and place one foot, then the other, on top of a Swiss ball. With your body in one straight line, your arms at a 90-degree angle, hands close together, bend your elbows and lower your chest to the floor.

273 Wide Push-Up

Balance your body with your arms wide apart. Slowly lower into your Push-Up. Be sure to keep the arms moving up and down, while hugging in along the sides of your body for optimal balance.

274 Medicine Ball Decline Push-Up

Begin on your hands and knees, with your hands about shoulder width apart. Balance your toes on a Medicine ball. With your body in one straight line, your arms at a 90-degree angle, hands close together, bend your elbows and lower your chest to the floor.

275 Balance Ball Travelling Push-Up

Start with your right hand on the floor and the left on top of a balance ball. Lower into your Push-Up, then bring both hands to the top of the ball. Put your left hand onto the floor, and keep your right arm on the balance ball. Lower into your Push-Up and then rise.

276 Balance Ball Push-Up with Glute Lift

This dynamic Push-Up gives you a good dose of balance and coordination work! Combining a Push-Up with the leg raise will develop strength throughout the upper body and abdominals. Performing this exercise requires the ability to secure the abs in tightly to the back while suspending your weight.

- Start in your Push-Up form with the hands each on the outside of the balance ball.
- Bend the arms into a Push-Up.
- Straighten up out of your Push-Up, and lift the left leg up into the air.
- Lower back into a Push-Up, and, extend back up, lifting the right leg.

Work Your Brain

Incorporating props into your workouts is a great way to enhance your balance and coordination work. Alternating props with your hands, from side to side, works the muscles in the body, but also works the brain's cross-axis circuits!

277 Plyometric Balance Ball Push-Up

This Push-Up variation maximizes force with its quick intervals between moves. And incorporating the balance ball creates an unstable base for your body. Start with a balance ball flipped over with the rounded side down and the flat side up.

- Start in your Push-Up form with the hands on either side of the flat side of a balance ball.
- Engage the arms and abdominals deeply into the core.
- Bend the arms into a Push-Up, quickly straighten the arms, and hold the body at the top.

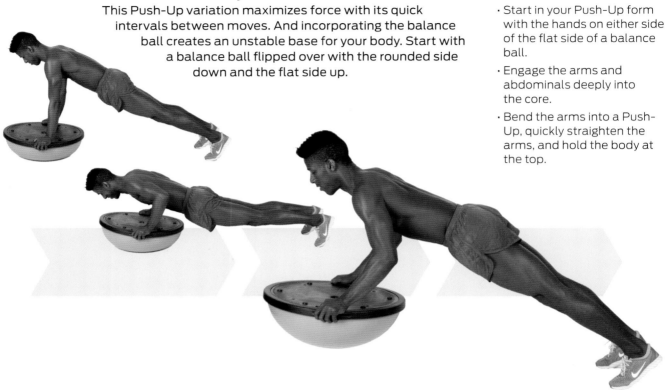

278 Flat Balance Ball Push-Up

The balance ball creates an unstable base for your body in Push-Up. Start with a balance ball flipped over with the rounded side down and the flat side up. Engage your abs strongly, squeeze the inner leg muscles together, with your hands in the middle of the balance ball. Balancing, perform a Push-Up.

279 Balance Ball Diamond Push-Up

With your palms down on the balance ball, extend your two thumb tips down and index fingers to touch, making a diamond shape. Slowly press the elbows open into your Push-Up. The closeness of your hands works the pecs and triceps.

280 Foam Roller Push-Up

Balance your body with your arms on a horizontal foam roller. Squeezing the upper arms into the sides of your body, slowly lower into your Push-Up. Be sure to keep the arms moving up and down along the sides of your body for optimal balance.

281 Foam Roller Push-Up and Walk Over

Start with your right hand on the floor and the left on top of a foam roller. Lower into your Push-Up, then bring both hands to the top of the roller. Put your left hand onto the floor, and keep your right hand on the roller. Lower into your Push-Up and then rise.

282 Medicine Ball Push-Up

Balancing your weight onto the ball with straight arms, perform a Push-Up in this position, keeping your balance by pulling the abs in deeply and working the arms slowly from bent to straight.

283 Swiss Ball Push-Up

By incorporating the Swiss ball into your Push-Up, you will maximize muscle intelligence and agility. The Swiss ball adds the challenge of instability, challenging all the muscles in the body to engage and pull up.

- Come into your Push-Up stance (#266).
- Walk your ankles onto the top of the Swiss ball. Squeeze your abs in strongly to support your balance here.
- Lengthen the spine and bend at the elbows, coming into your Push-Up, bringing your chest close to the floor. Straighten the arms and repeat.

284 Swiss Ball Incline Dumbbell Press

Come to your hands and knees, and place each hand on a dumbbell. Place one foot, then the other, on top of a Swiss ball. With your body in one straight line, your arms at a 90-degree angle, hands closely together, bend your elbows and lower your chest to the floor.

285 Knee Push-Up and Roll-Out

Hold on to a barbell with round weights at either end, and place both knees together on the floor. Lower out into your Push-Up while extending the torso long, keeping the arms straight, and rolling the barbell away from your body. Roll back up to the starting position.

286 Push-Up and Roll-Out

Hold your barbell while in a balanced Push-Up stance. Lower out into your Push-Up while extending the torso long, keeping the arms straight, rolling the barbell away from your body. Allow the chest to come as close to the floor as you can manage! Roll back up to the starting position.

287 Push-Up and Roll-Out Dumbbell Variation

Holding your dumbbells, come into your Push-Up stance (#266). With a long spine and very straight arms, bend your elbows slowly into a Push-Up. Hold low in Push-Up and take turns alternating rolling out, extending the dumbbells straight in front of you, and bringing them back in.

288 Suspended Push-Up

Come to your hands and knees and place one foot, then the other, into the suspension strap. With your body in one straight line, your arms at a 90-degree angle, hands shoulder width, bend your elbows and lower your chest to the floor. Push back up and repeat.

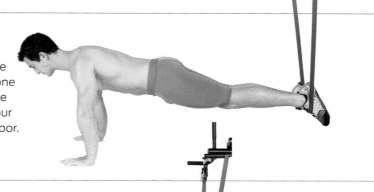

289 Suspended Atomic Push-Up

With your feet suspended off the ground in your strap, hold the arms very long and strong at a 90-degree angle to your body. Keep your upper body straight and engage the upper abs to pull your legs into your chest. Hold there for an added challenge and then push back out!

290 Towel Fly Push-Up

The Towel Fly is an advance modification of the Push-Up that calls for you to move your arms in and out rather than up and down. Assume the upright Push-Up position, with your hands on a towel on a smooth floor. Keeping your torso rigid, slide your hands together, bunching the towel, and slide back. Repeat.

291 Medicine Ball Walkover

Start with your right hand on the floor and the left on top of your Medicine ball. Lower into your Push-Up, then bring both hands to the top of the ball. Put your left hand onto the floor, and keep your right arm on the ball. Lower into your Push-Up and then rise.

CHAPTER TWO

Static Exercises

Static exercises are routines or movements in which the muscles in the body move little or in very small amounts, yet receive huge results. Most static exercises can also be referred to as "isometric." You have probably done a few of these kinds of movements before, at some point. Some of the more well known static exercises, which we will delve into in the following pages, are balances, planks, and bridges. Widely recognized body-meditation related practices, including yoga, Pilates, Gyrotonics, the Feldenkrais Method, tai chi, various martial arts systems, and ballet—among other dance forms—all contain a myriad of isometric/static movements. Combine a few of these moves into your routine to develop deep muscular endurance, muscle tone, and strength!

292

Single Leg Balance

When you bring your knee up to hip height, and isometrically hold it in place, you are engaging your core and all the muslces in the body, isometrically. Additionally, you are giving the lower back a stretch down through the hamstring. Alternating the knees up into the chest, while holding in a balance, will develop agility, flexibility, and core strength. Try to visualize your balances as full-body movements, activating every muscle into the experience.

Annotation Key
Bold text indicates target muscles
Black text indicates other working muscles
* indicates deep muscles

Correct form
Keep the back long and upright. Keep the abs glued into the lower back to support the core.

Avoid
Do not let the shoulders hunch forward, or open too far behind you. Keep your abdominals engaged for proper alignment.

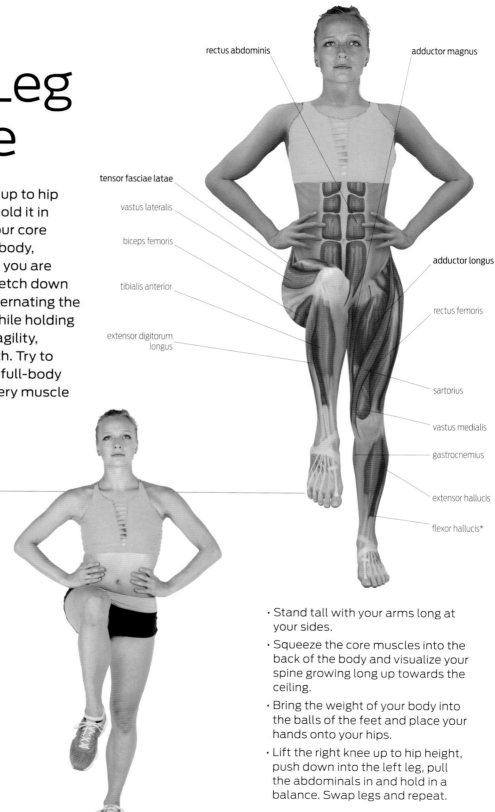

rectus abdominis

adductor magnus

tensor fasciae latae

vastus lateralis

biceps femoris

tibialis anterior

extensor digitorum longus

adductor longus

rectus femoris

sartorius

vastus medialis

gastrocnemius

extensor hallucis

flexor hallucis*

- Stand tall with your arms long at your sides.
- Squeeze the core muscles into the back of the body and visualize your spine growing long up towards the ceiling.
- Bring the weight of your body into the balls of the feet and place your hands onto your hips.
- Lift the right knee up to hip height, push down into the left leg, pull the abdominals in and hold in a balance. Swap legs and repeat.

293 Inverted Hamstring

Start standing upright with the arms extended overhead. Step forward onto the left leg and stretch the right leg out behind you. Open your arms out to the sides to help you with your balance. Keep the head, torso, and leg all in one straight line for an advanced balance. Repeat on the other side.

294 Inverted Hamstring with Weights

Start standing upright with the arms extended overhead, holding your weights. Step forward onto the right leg and stretch the left leg out behind you. Open your arms out to behind you to help you with your balance. Keep the head, torso, and leg all in one straight line. Swap sides and repeat.

295 One-Legged Chair Pose

Start standing upright with the arms extended overhead. Lift the right leg off the ground and, with the leg raised, tip the hips back, and lower slowly into a One-Legged Chair Pose. Take care of your bending knee by strongly engaging the abs the whole time! Repeat with the left leg raised.

296 Single Leg Circles

Single Leg Circles is an exercise done while lying flush with the floor. The aim of the exercise is to move slowly, bringing your leg around and around in small circle shapes, while stabilizing all the little muscles in and around the pelvis and hip joint. You can perform small circles to start, and then gradually make bigger circles as you advance.

- Lie flat on the floor with both legs long, keeping the arms at your sides, pushing the palms into the ground.
- Bring your left leg up, directly over your left hip.
- Cross the leg to the right shoulder, across the body, then, sweep it down to the right foot. Continue your circle, moving the leg outside of the right foot, then back up to the starting position.
- Reverse the circle of the leg, starting out to the left first. Switch legs and repeat.

297 Leg Front Pull

Mastering the Leg Front Pull is something that takes time. Each of us has a different range, agility, and flexibility. As a beginner, if you are struggling to get the Leg Front Pull straight, start out with two bent knees and then graduate to extending the legs. Incorporating a strap or band of some sort can be very helpful as well.

- Stand up straight with both legs slightly bent at the knees.
- Bring the weight of your body into the balls of the feet.
- Lift the right knee up to hip height, push down into the left leg, and pull the abdominals in.
- Reach both hands for the right ankle, and slowly extend the right leg long and straight.
- Switch legs and repeat.

298 Tree Pose

Bring both legs in close to touch. Squeeze your inner thighs tightly together and bring the weight of your body into the balls of your feet. Reach down and pull your right foot up, bending it into your left knee. Press your foot against the inner knee and extend the arms overhead. Switch legs and repeat.

299 Sideways Tree Pose

Bring both legs in close to touch. Squeeze your inner thighs tightly together and bring the weight of your body into the balls of your feet. Reach down and pull your right foot up, bending it into your left knee. Press your foot against the inner knee, extend the arms out to your sides and tilt the torso to the right, looking left. Switch sides and repeat.

300

Upward Lotus Tree Pose

Bring both legs in close to touch. Squeeze your inner thighs tightly together and bring the weight of your body into the balls of your feet. Reach down with your left hand and pull your right foot up, bending it across the top of your left knee. Press your right foot against the left leg and extend the right arm up. Switch sides.

301

Hand to Foot, Hand to Knee Tree Pose

Stand with your feet together. Bend your right knee, and reach down with your right arm. Take the outside of your right knee with the right hand and press it up high behind you, bending the torso forward slightly. Reach around to the left with the left hand and grasp the top of the right foot. Switch sides.

302

Extended Pose

Bring the weight of your body into the balls of the feet. Lift the right knee up to hip height, push down into the left leg, and pull the abdominals in. Reach both hands for the right ankle, extend the right leg long and straight, and pull it up to your face. Switch legs and repeat.

303

Extended Hand to Big Toe

Bring both legs in close to touch. Squeeze your inner thighs tightly together and bring the weight of your body into the balls of your feet. Reach down and pull your left foot up, bending it into your right knee. Take the big toe of your left foot into your left hand and extend it open to the side. Switch legs and repeat.

304

Revolved Extended Hand to Big Toe

Bring the weight of your body into the balls of the feet. Lift the right knee up to hip height, push down into the left leg, and pull the abdominals in. Reach your left hand for the inside of the right foot, extend the right leg long and straight to the left, twisting the torso right. Switch sides.

305

Thigh Rock-Back

These rock-backs focus the bulk of work into your quads, inner thighs, hamstrings, and glute muscles. By kneeling and isolating the knee joint to bend deeply, hinging the weight of your body back into space, behind your center plunge line, you engage all the muscles in your core and lower legs deeply!

rectus abdominis

tensor fasciae latae

sartorius

vastus intermedius*

rectus femoris

vastus lateralis

vastus medialis

gluteus maximus

adductor magnus

biceps femoris

Annotation Key
Bold text indicates target muscles
Black text indicates other working muscles
* indicates deep muscles

Correct form
Keep the body in one line from the knees to the top of the head, on both the front and back sides of the body!

Avoid
Do not allow the thighs to grip, straining the quad muscles. Keep your muscles long and still.

- Kneel on top of a soft surface, with your knees slightly apart in a hip-width stance.
- Let your arms hang at the sides of your body.
- Lengthen your spine long, pull your abdominals in toward your lower back.
- Squeeze your butt muscles and hamstrings, and allow the weight of your body to lean back into the space behind you.
- Squeeze the legs and core to bring you back up straight.

306 Thigh Rock-Back with Plate

In order to achieve your maximum rock-back you must squeeze the abs in to support the lower back and hamstrings. This exercise can be made more challenging by adding weight onto the front of the hips.

- Kneel on top of a soft surface, with your knees slightly apart in a hip-width stance. Bring a weighted plate just below your chest.
- Lengthen your spine long, pull your abdominals in toward your lower back.
- Squeeze your butt muscles and hamstrings, and allow the weight of your body to lean back into the space behind you.
- Squeeze the legs and core to bring you back up straight.

307 Thigh Rock-Back with Raised Dumbbells

Kneel on top of a soft surface, with your knees slightly apart in a hip-width stance. Hold your dumbbells out in front of the chest. Lengthen your spine long, pull your abdominals in toward your lower back. Squeeze your butt muscles and hamstrings, and allow the weight of your body to lean back into the space behind you, and twist to the right, then left.

308 Thigh Rock-Back and Twist

With your knees slightly apart in a hip-width stance, hold your dumbbells out in front of the chest. Lengthen your spine long, pull your abdominals in toward your lower back. Squeeze your butt muscles and hamstrings, lean back into the space behind you, and twist to the right, then left.

309 Thigh Rock-Back with Medicine Ball

With your knees slightly apart in a hip-width stance, hold your Medicine ball into the front of the chest. Lengthen your spine long, pull your abdominals in toward your lower back. Squeeze your butt muscles and hamstrings, lean back into the space behind you, and twist to the right, then left.

Fire Hydrant

Correct form
Keep your back flat by pulling in the abdominals deeply towards the lower back.

Avoid
Do not position the knees in or out further than a 90 degree angle. Square alignment is key in this set of movements.

This variation of core exercise can be found in almost all abdominal-focused workouts like yoga, Pilates, ballet barre, and calisthenics. The focus is on keeping the core stabilized between two hands and one leg, while you lift and lower the other leg to the side, working the inner and outer muscles of the hip and glutes.

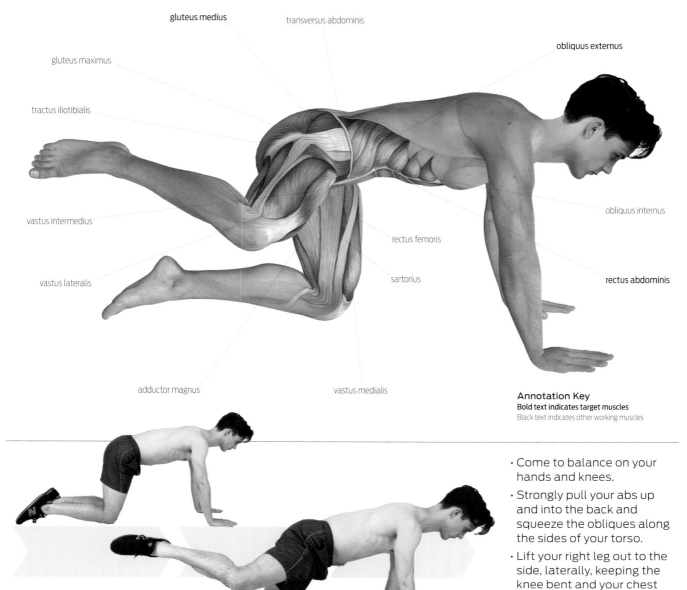

gluteus medius

transversus abdominis

obliquus externus

gluteus maximus

tractus iliotibialis

obliquus internus

vastus intermedius

rectus femoris

vastus lateralis

sartorius

rectus abdominis

adductor magnus

vastus medialis

Annotation Key
Bold text indicates target muscles
Black text indicates other working muscles

- Come to balance on your hands and knees.
- Strongly pull your abs up and into the back and squeeze the obliques along the sides of your torso.
- Lift your right leg out to the side, laterally, keeping the knee bent and your chest facing the ground. Swap legs and repeat.

311 Straight Leg Fire Hydrant

Begin with the weight centered between your hands and knees. Engage your legs and abs, squeezing the obliques in along the sides of your torso. Lift your right leg out to the side with the knee bent, and extend the leg to a straight position. Switch legs and repeat.

312 Fire Hydrant In-Out

Isolating the work of one leg at a time from this four-post position, on the hands and knees, is a great way to use the body's own weight in building core strength. You can do these leg isolations anywhere you see fit. Come to balance on your hands and knees. Strongly pull your abs up and into the back, and squeeze the obliques along the sides of your torso. Lift your right leg out to the side, and push the leg to extend back behind you. Switch legs and repeat.

313 Fire Hydrant with Leg Weights

Begin with the weight centered between your hands and knees. Secure a leg weight at the upper ankle on your left leg. Engage your abs, squeezing the obliques in along the sides of your torso. Lift your left leg out to the side with the knee bent, and extend the leg to a straight position. Transfer the weight to your right upper ankle and repeat on the right side.

314 Weighted Bird Dog

Secure a leg weight at the upper ankle on your left leg. With the weight evenly placed on both hands and knees, raise the right arm off the floor, straight out in front of you. Then raise the left leg, straight out behind you. Pull the abs in deeply and stretch from right hand to left leg in your balance. Swap sides and the weight and repeat.

315 Pointer

Assume the plank position, and then extend your left arm straight forward while raising your right leg until your whole body forms a straight line from toe to shoulder. Pause at the top of the movement and lower back to the plank position. Repeat on the other side.

316 Roller Knee Pull-In

Balance in your standard plank with your arms extended and palms down. Walk your feet onto your foam roller, bend at the hips, and roll your knees into the chest. Suck your core up into your lower back and hold in your curved-in position.

317 Arm Leg Extension

Lie face down on the floor with your arms bent in front of your chest and the legs long. Pull the abs up into the back, lift the left leg off the floor, and simultaneously reach the right arm forward and up. Alternate arms and legs.

318 Raised Arm Leg Extension

Extend your body long on top of a yoga mat. Bring your arms close together overhead and bring your legs to touch, squeezing the inner thighs tightly. Engage the abs strongly, and in one move lift your arms and legs off the floor together.

319 Medicine Ball Extension

Start with your Medicine ball centered on the lower back. With the weight evenly placed on both hands and knees, raise the right arm off the floor, straight out in front of you. Then raise the left leg, straight out behind you. Pull the abs in deeply and stretch from right hand to left leg in your balance. Swap sides and repeat.

320 Plank Arm Leg Extension

Bring your forearms open in your plank. Extend the legs long, and put the weight onto the balls of your feet. Squeeze the abs in and extend the right arm forward while picking up the left leg. Keep the left forearm down and into the ground. Swap sides and repeat.

321 Swiss Ball Pike

The Swiss Ball Pike is a great combination of planking and isometric abdominal work. Utilizing your Swiss ball as a moving prop for the lower body to manipulate, you will strengthen your abdominal wall and stabilize the pelvis, while also creating power in the arms to balance in a semi-handstand position.

- Start in a solid plank position with your feet supported at the center of your Swiss ball.
- Engage the lower abs and the lower back and bend at the hips.
- Allow the Swiss ball to roll in toward the body, and pike the hips up high into the sky.
- Hold at the top of your pike by pulling in the abdominals deeply.

Total Core

Working your core and learning to stabilize from there will determine the success of your exercises. One tip is to visualize your core as having a wrapping motion, starting from your abdominals and pulling around into your lower back.

322 Swiss Ball Walk-Around

Come into your long plank position with the arms fully extended and feet supported at the center of your Swiss ball. Bend at the hips and pike the lower body up high into the air. Hold in your pike position, pull in the abs strongly, and move the hands toward the right and then the left, then return to a plank.

323 Swiss Ball Forward Roll-Out

Bring the weight of your upper body into your forearms while balancing on the Swiss ball. Lower the knees down in an extended kneeling position. Push the forearms into the ball and squeeze the abs very deeply, rolling the ball out away from you.

324 Swiss Ball Transverse Abs

Work the deepest layer of the core in this plank variation. Bring the weight of your upper body into your forearms while balancing on the Swiss ball. Push the forearms into the ball and squeeze the abs very deeply.

325 Swiss Ball Band Extension

Begin in your forearm plank, supported on the Swiss ball. With a secure band around the lower calves, extend the legs long and flex the feet. Squeeze the abs in and take turns pressing out against the band with each leg.

326 Medicine Ball Pike Up

Start in a plank with your feet supported on top of a Medicine ball. Engage the lower abs and the lower back and bend at the hips. Allow the ball to roll in toward the body, and pike the hips up high into the sky. Hold at the top of your pike by pulling in the abdominals deeply.

327 Swiss Ball Plow

Lie with your back long against the floor. Bring your calves onto the Swiss ball. Push your hips up to the ceiling, come up high onto the backs of the shoulders, and bend your knees over your head. Hold the Swiss ball with your arms extended behind you and stretch the legs out long.

328 Swiss Ball Plow with Abduction

Start lying flush with the floor on your back. Place the Swiss ball up high, between the ankles. Squeeze in on the ball with your inner thighs, and rock the lower body back over the top of the head. Push down into the floor with the arms behind you.

329 Swiss Ball Skier

Performing this plank variation involves simultaneously shifting the weight of the lower extremities side to side while stabilizing the core muscle groups, and the full extension of the arm, hip, and pelvic muscles.

- Bring your body into an extended plank with a Swiss ball under your knees.
- Squeeze the abs in, up, and away from the floor underneath you.
- Lengthen the spine by reaching the top of your head away from your feet.
- Shift the hips open to the right, and then to the left.

Bridge

Correct form
Your body should be in a straight line from head to knee when you are at the top of your Bridge.

Avoid
Do not bring the feet in too close to the bottom. Make sure there is enough space to bridge up and down with ease.

Bridging activates all of the muscles in the lower and upper legs. In order to achieve your maximum Bridge you must squeeze the abs in to support the lower back and hamstrings. Bridges can be made more challenging by adding weight onto the front of the hips and/or lifting one leg off of the floor.

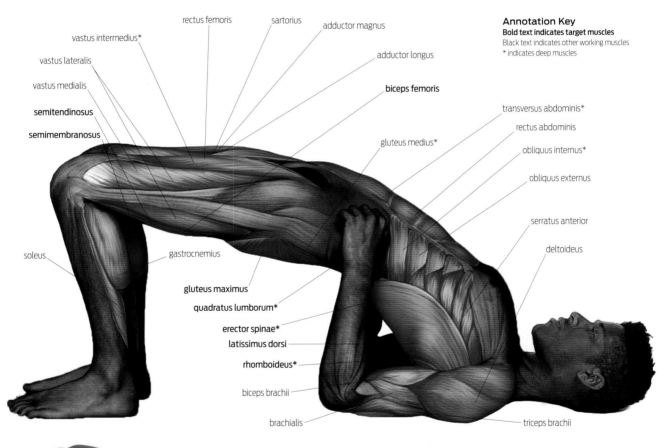

Annotation Key
Bold text indicates target muscles
Black text indicates other working muscles
* indicates deep muscles

rectus femoris
sartorius
adductor magnus
vastus intermedius*
adductor longus
vastus lateralis
biceps femoris
vastus medialis
transversus abdominis*
semitendinosus
rectus abdominis
semimembranosus
gluteus medius*
obliquus internus*
obliquus externus
serratus anterior
deltoideus
soleus
gastrocnemius
gluteus maximus
quadratus lumborum*
erector spinae*
latissimus dorsi
rhomboideus*
biceps brachii
brachialis
triceps brachii

- Lie with your back long against the floor. Engage the abs so that they are pulled deeply into the lower back.
- Bring your feet to the floor and squeeze your inner thighs together.
- Press into your arms along the sides of the body and lift the hips high into the air. Engage the core and hamstrings at the top of your Bridge.

331 Bridge with Plate

Lie with your back long on the floor. Bring your feet to the floor and squeeze your inner thighs together. Place a weight on top of the hips. Lift the hips high into the air. Engage the core deeply.

332 Bridge with Leg Lift

Lie with your back long on the floor. Bring your feet to the floor and squeeze your inner thighs together. Extend your right leg up toward the ceiling with the knee bent. Lift the hips high into the air by engaging the hamstrings and core strongly. Extend your right leg up toward the ceiling. Return your right foot and hips to the floor. Raise your left leg and repeat.

333 Bridge with 90-Degree Leg Lift

When performing your leg lifts, be sure to really engage the abs deeply and firmly. Bridges with leg lifts are all about finding the balance of weight between the arms, pelvis, and extended leg. The higher your hips bridge, the more you must stabilize your core.

- Lie with your back long on the floor.
- Extend your right leg up toward the ceiling and stretch it in toward the torso.
- Lift the hips high into the air by engaging the hamstrings and core strongly.
- Return your right foot and hips to the floor.
- Raise the left leg to 90-degrees and repeat.

334 Piriformis Bridge

Lie on your back and bend your knees, bringing the feet to the floor. Place the right ankle on top of left knee. Squeeze your glutes and lift the hips high into the air by engaging the hamstrings and core strongly. Press the arms into the floor for an added stretch. Swap legs and repeat.

335 Suspended Bridge

Lie with your back long on the floor. Bring your heels into a set of secure suspension straps. Push down with the arms at your sides and lift the hips high into the air. Take care to keep pressing down firmly into your shoulders and upper arms for support.

336 Aerobic Step Bridge with Leg Lift and Chest Press

Step your feet up onto a low box and bring your body in toward the box, with your hips about 1 foot (30 cm) from the edge. Bend your knees. Hold your dumbbells and bring them into your chest. Extend your right leg long to the ceiling, press your hips up into a Bridge, and push your weights out from the chest. Repeat, using the left leg.

337 One Leg Balance Ball Bridge

Lie with your back long on the floor. Bring your feet to the rounded side of a balance ball and squeeze your inner thighs together. Lift the hips high into the air by engaging the hamstrings and core strongly. Extend your right leg up toward the ceiling. Repeat, raising the left leg.

338 Swiss Ball Bridge Reverse Rotation

Come to balance with your middle back supported on a Swiss ball. Bend the knees and push the hips up to hover off the floor. With your torso long, reach your Medicine ball out from the chest. Twist to the left and then to the right.

339 Swiss Ball Reverse Bridge Roll

Come to balance with your whole torso supported on a Swiss ball. Bend the knees and push the hips up to hover off the floor. With your torso long, reach your weighted ball out from the chest. Twist to the left and then to the right, keeping the legs still.

340 Swiss Ball Sit to Bridge

This is a great variation for opening up the upper chest and stretching the spine, abdominals, and pelvis. Essentially, moving through this exercise will assist you in learning how to place your body in alignment for a full-body bridge or a "wheel" as they would call it in yoga.

- Start sitting up long on a Swiss ball. Extend your arms out from the chest in front of you.
- Slowly, roll your lower spine down onto the ball, then your shoulders and upper back.
- Reach your arms for the ground behind you.
- When your hands have reached the floor above you, push into the feet and legs and raise the hips up away from the ball.

341 Swiss Ball Bridge

Start sitting in front of the Swiss ball. Open the arms, and slowly push your lower spine up on to the ball, then your shoulders and upper back. Reach your arms wide to the sides and push your hips up into a full Bridge.

342 Swiss Ball Leg Bridge

Lie with your back long on the floor. Bring your heels up onto the Swiss ball. Push down with the arms at your sides and lift the hips high into the air, bridging with legs straight. Take care to keep pressing down firmly into your shoulders and upper arms for support.

343 Swiss Ball Leg Bridge with Leg Raises

Lie with your back long on the floor. Bring your heels up onto the Swiss ball. Push down with the arms at your sides and lift the hips high into the air, bridging. Dig your heels into the Swiss ball and alternate lifting and lowering each leg up off of the ball.

344 Swiss Ball Bridge with Leg Curl

When performing your leg curls, be sure to really engage the abs deeply and firmly. Curls on the Swiss ball are all about finding the balance of weight between the arms, pelvis, and feet. The higher your hips bridge, the more you must stabilize your core.

- Lie with your back long on the floor.
- Bring your heels up onto the Swiss ball.
- Push down with the arms at your sides, straighten the knees, and lift the hips high into the air, bridging.
- Take care to keep pressing down firmly into your shoulders and upper arms for support.
- Bend the knees, moving the ball toward your body and then away.

345 Swiss Ball Table Top Rotation

Lie supine in tabletop position with a Swiss ball between your knees. Press your shoulders into the floor and move your hips, legs and the Swiss ball to your left. Try to keep your torso still. Return to the starting position and repeat to the right.

346 Swiss Ball Bridge Curl Up

Lie with your back long against the floor. Engage the abs so that they are pulled deeply into the lower back, and bring your calves onto the Swiss ball. Squeeze your inner thighs together, press into your arms along the sides of the body, and come into a crunch.

347 Backward Ball Stretch

This is a great stretch for the upper chest, spine, abdominals, and pelvis. The Backward Ball Stretch will assist you in learning how to place your body in alignment for a full-body bridge or a "wheel" as they would call it in yoga.

- Start sitting up long on a Swiss ball. Extend your arms out from your shoulders, keeping them slightly bent.
- Slowly, roll your lower spine down onto the ball, then your shoulders and upper back.
- Reach your arms for the ground behind you.
- When your forearms have reached the ground, breathe deeply and relax into the stretch.

348 Foam Roller Bridge with Leg Lift 1

Lie with your back long on the floor. Bring a foam roller under your shoulders, and extend the legs long. Push the heels into the floor, lift the hips high into the air by engaging the hamstrings and core strongly, and raise your right leg out from the hip. Repeat and raise the left leg.

349 Foam Roller Bridge with Leg Lift 2

Lie with your back long on the floor. Bring your feet to the top side of a foam roller and squeeze your inner thighs together. Lift the hips high into the air by engaging the hamstrings and core strongly. Extend your right leg up toward the ceiling, then the left.

350 Moving Bridge

Engage the abs so that they are pulled deeply into the lower back. Bring your feet to the floor and squeeze your inner thighs together. Lift the hips high into the air, coming into a Bridge. Extend your right leg off the floor, then bend it and lower down. Alternate sides.

351 Hamstring Pull In

Lie on your back along the floor and bring your feet up onto the top of a foam roller. Squeeze the core in deeply, engage your hamstrings, and press your hips up into a Bridge. Keeping your arms long at your sides, roll the foam roller in toward your hips, working the hamstrings.

352

Plank

The Plank is a core exercise that can be found in almost all abdominal-focused workouts like yoga, Pilates, ballet barre, and calisthenics. Planking is all about keeping the core stabilized, suspended in the air, balancing on two arms and the balls of the feet. Not only does it strengthen the core muscle groups, but it's also great for stabilizing the lower back and aiding with back pain.

Correct form
Keep proper alignment in your plank by imagining that your body is reaching away from the core in both directions.

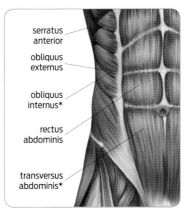

Annotation Key
Bold text indicates target muscles
Black text indicates other working muscles
* indicates deep muscles

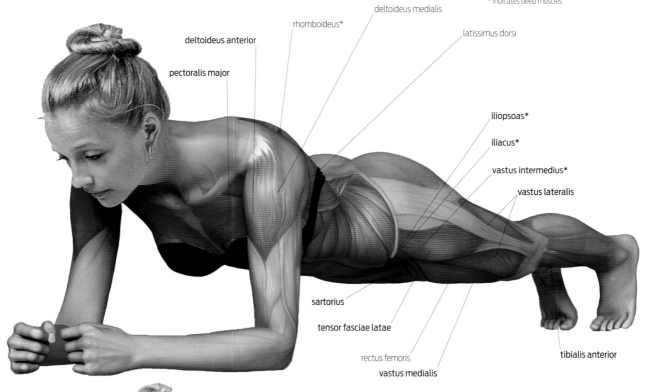

serratus anterior
obliquus externus
obliquus internus*
rectus abdominis
transversus abdominis*

deltoideus medialis
rhomboideus*
deltoideus anterior
pectoralis major
latissimus dorsi
iliopsoas*
iliacus*
vastus intermedius*
vastus lateralis
sartorius
tensor fasciae latae
rectus femoris
vastus medialis
tibialis anterior

Avoid
Do not tense the neck or shoulders by trying to lift the focus of the eyes up further than you need to. Keep your gaze down and soft.

- Bring your body to balance on your forearms and the balls of your feet.
- Squeeze the abs in deeply, up, and away from the floor underneath you.
- Lengthen the spine by reaching the top of your head away from your feet.

353 Simple Plank

Bring your body to balance on your forearms and your knees. Squeeze the abs in deeply, up and away from the floor underneath you. Lengthen the spine by reaching the top of your head away from your knees, and bring your thighs down toward the floor.

354 Plank Press-Up

Bring your body to balance on your forearms and the balls of your feet. Squeeze the abs in deeply, up and away from the floor underneath you, and raise your butt and back up, keeping your feet and forearms in place. It will give a nice stretch in the back as well as strengthen the core.

355 Plank with Leg Lift

Planks are one of the most simple moves to do. They are excellent for building up those deep inner core muscles that provide stability for your lower back. Planks are also excellent for improving posture, balance, and reducing back pain.

- Start with your abs pulled up and in, kneeling on the floor.
- With the weight evenly placed on both hands and knees, raise the right arm off the floor, straight out in front of you.
- Then, raise the left leg straight out behind you. Pull the abs in deeply and stretch from right hand to left leg in your balance. Swap sides and repeat.

356 Forearm Plank with Knee Drops

Bring your body to balance on your forearms and the balls of your feet. Squeeze the abs in deeply, up and away from the floor underneath you. Pull the abs up into the lower back and alternate dropping each knee to the floor.

357 Low Plank Challenge

Bring your body into a very low plank. Squeeze the abs in deeply, up and away from the floor underneath you. Lengthen the spine by reaching the top of your head away from your feet. Isolate the elbows, bending them along your sides. Hug the elbows in at the bottom of this move.

358 Suspended Forearm Plank

Come into a plank with your forearms supporting you. Push down with your forearms into the floor and take turns bringing your left foot to sit behind your right knee, then your right foot to sit behind your left knee.

359 Spiderman Plank

Come into a plank with your forearms supporting you. Push down into the floor with your forearms and pull your core in tightly. Take turns bringing your left knee to your left elbow, then your right knee to your right elbow.

360 Arm-Reach Plank

Bring your body to balance on your forearms and the balls of your feet. Squeeze the abs in deeply, up and away from the floor underneath you. Lengthen the spine by reaching the top of your head away from your feet. Reach the right arm out to the side, then your left arm.

361 Plank-Up

Bring your body to balance on your forearms and the balls of your feet. Squeeze the abs in deeply, up and away from the floor underneath you. Extend your right arm up vertically, resting on the left. Hold here, then swap and perform on the other side.

362 Plank Roll-Down

This Plank Roll-Down is great for stabilizing the core and the lower back. If you have issues with lower back pain, this is the move for you! By utilizing a segment-by-segment roll-down pattern, through the spine and coming into a plank, you will create strong abs that support the whole core.

· Start standing with the legs in a wide shoulder-width position.
· Bend at the hips and reach your hands to the floor.
· Walk each palm out further forward and away from the feet.
· When you have reached a plank position hold there.
· Walk back in and repeat.

Ab and Ad Some

Anatomically speaking, the word "abduction" applies to the movement of one body part away from the midline of the body. Adduction infers the opposite: one part of the body moving in toward the body's midline.

363 Plank Press

Bring your body to balance on your forearms and the balls of your feet. Squeeze the abs in deeply, up and away from the floor underneath you. Pull the abs up into the lower back and press firmly down into the floor with both hands flat.

364 Short Plank

Bring your body to balance on your hands and knees. Squeeze the abs in deeply, up and away from the floor underneath you. Lengthen the spine by reaching the top of your head away from your feet.

365 Plank Knee Pull-In

Come into an upright straight armed plank. Engage the core deeply and bend your left knee into the center of the chest, between the arms. In one move push the left leg out high to the back. Alternate sides and pick up the tempo bringing the knees in quickly for added cardio.

366 High Plank

Incorporating High Planks into your workout routine is a great way to stabilize the core and strengthen the entire body through isometrics. High Planks can be done in conjunction with balance balls, raised surfaces, Swiss balls—just about anywhere! Add weight to your planking routine for an added challenge.

- Bring your body to balance on your hands and the balls of your feet in an extended arm plank.
- Squeeze the abs in deeply, up and away from the floor underneath you.
- Lengthen the spine by reaching the top of your head away from your feet.

367 High Plank with Leg Extension

Bring your body into an extended arm plank. Extend the legs long, and put the weight onto the balls of your feet. Squeeze the abs in a lot and extend the spine forward while picking up the right leg. Keep your core tight as you alternate your legs.

368 High Plank with Knee Pull-In

Balance in your High Plank with your palms open to shoulder width. Squeeze the core deeply and bend your right knee into the chest. Stay high in the plank and alternate sides, bringing the left knee into the chest.

369 High Plank with Jacks Variation

Start in your plank with the legs and arms extended long. Put the weight in your hands, squeeze the abs in, and jump your feet open to a wide shoulder-width position. Jump the legs back together, and repeat.

370 Low to High Plank

Balance your body with your arms in a High Plank. Squeeze the upper arms into the sides of your body and slowly lower into your low plank. Be sure to keep the arms moving up and down along the sides of your body for optimal balance.

371 Four-Limbed Staff Pose Preparation

Bring your body to balance on your hands and the balls of your feet in a High Plank. Squeeze the abs in deeply, up and away from the floor underneath you. Track the upper arm and biceps in towards the chest, lowering the body and bending the elbows slightly.

372 Upward Plank

Performing planks that simultaneously bring the lower extremities in to meet the upper body are a great challenge and require you to stabilize the core muscle groups and also the hip and pelvis muscles.

- With your legs long out in front of you, place your hands down at your hips.
- Dig your heels into the ground and push your hips up into a reverse plank.
- Keeping the weight balanced between your hands and heels, pushing the hips up high.

373 Upward Plank with Leg Lift

With your legs long out in front of you, place your hands down at your hips. Dig your heels into the ground and push your hips up into a reverse plank. Keeping the weight balanced between your hands and heels, take turns kicking each leg up to the sky.

374 Upward Plank Hip Lift

With your legs long out in front of you, place your hands down behind you on an elevated box. Dig your heels into the ground and push your hips up into a reverse plank, with knees bent. Keeping the weight balanced between your hands and heels, lower and lift the hips.

375 Upward Plank March

With your legs long out in front of you, place your hands down behind the hips. Dig your heels into the ground and push your hips up into a reverse plank, with knees bent. Keeping the weight balanced between your hands and heels, lower and lift the legs.

376 Side Plank

Begin sitting on the right hip. Place your right hand on the floor and push your hips up, coming into a Side Plank. Let your left arm rest on the left thigh. Take turns sitting and pushing up into your Side Plank. Swap sides and repeat.

377 Forearm Side Plank

Begin sitting on the right hip. Place your right forearm on the floor and push your hips up, coming into a Side Plank. Let your left hand come to the hip. Take turns sitting and pushing up into your Side Plank. Swap sides and repeat.

378 Forearm Side Plank with Hip Raise on Step

Begin sitting on the right hip. Stack your feet onto an elevated box and place your right forearm on the floor. Push your hips up, coming into a Side Plank on the box. Rest your left hand on your hip. Take turns sitting and pushing up into your Side Plank. Swap sides.

379

Forearm Side Plank with Knee Tuck

Begin sitting on the right hip. Reach your right forearm out along the floor and push your hips up, coming into a Side Plank. Let your left arm come to the hip. Bend your left knee up into the chest and lower down back into a Side Plank. Swap sides and repeat.

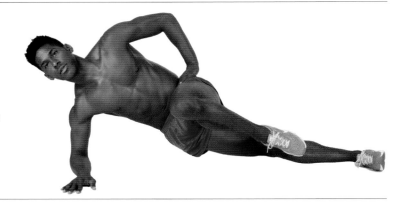

380

Foam Roller Plank

Start with your feet propped up on the foam roller. Bring your palms to the floor and come into your plank by extending the legs long, balancing the weight onto the balls of your feet and hands. Squeeze the abs in strongly!

381

Rolling Planks

Start kneeling and come to balance in your High Plank with the hands on the top of the foam roller. Bring the weight of your body forward into your hands and suck the core in tight to your spine. Bend your knees, and roll your body back to kneel.

382

Foam Roller Plank on Hands

Start with your spine stretching long. Bring your hands to balance on top of the foam roller. Come into your plank by extending the legs long, placing the the weight of the body up into the core and backs of the legs. Squeeze the abs in strongly!

383

Balance Ball Side Plank

Incorporating the balance ball into your plank routines is a great way to work on enhancing your body's natural sense of balance and stabilization. The balance ball acts as an unstable base, giving you the opportunity to really deepen the work of the core muscle groups.

- Place your right forearm down and into the center of your balance ball.
- Squeeze the obliques along the sides of the body and push up into a Side Plank with your body supported by your right arm.
- Lower the hips back down and take turns sitting and pushing up into your Side Plank. Swap sides and repeat.

384

Balance Ball Spiderman Plank

Place your balance ball with the flat side down. Come into a plank with your hands on the balance ball. Take turns bringing your right knee to your right elbow, then your left knee to your left elbow.

385

Balance Ball Forearm Plank

Start with your balance ball flat side down. Bring your forearms together with fingers clasped, on top and in the center of the balance ball. Come into your plank by extending the legs long, putting the weight onto the balls of your feet. Squeeze the abs in and hold!

386 Forearm Plank with Feet on a Balance Ball

Place the balance ball round side up. Come into a forearm plank position with your toes on the center of the balance ball. Keep your body in a straight line and hold for as long as you are able.

387 Balance Ball Side Plank with Lateral Shoulder Raise

Place your left forearm down and into the center of your balance ball. Push up into a Side Plank with your body supported by your left arm. Take a dumbbell in your right hand and open it up to your right side. Reach the dumbbell under your left ribs and then open back up. Repeat on the other side.

388 Single Leg Balance Ball Plank

Bring your body into an extended arm plank at the center of your balance ball. Extend the legs long, and put the weight onto the balls of your feet. Squeeze the abs in and extend the spine forward while picking up the right leg. Keep your core tight as your alternate legs.

389 Balance Ball Plank to Tap Out

Place the balance ball round side up. Come into a forearm plank position with the balls of your feet at the center of the balance ball. Keeping your body in one straight line, walk the right foot out to the side of the balance ball, then the left. Step the right foot, then the left foot back up onto the balance ball. Repeat as many times as you can!

390 Balance Ball Scissor Plank

Start with your balance ball flat side down. Bring your forearms together with fingers clasped, on top and in the center of the balance ball. Come into your plank by extending the legs long, putting the weight onto the balls of your feet. Step the feet out, then back in.

391 Balance Ball Side Plank with Leg Lift

Start with your balance ball flat side down. Place your left forearm on the balance ball and come into your Side Plank. Raise and lower your right leg to hip height. Swap sides and repeat.

392 Side Plank and Hip Raise with Arm on a Balance Ball

Begin sitting on the left hip. Place your left forearm into the balance ball and push your hips up, coming into a Side Plank. Let your right hand rest on the right hip. Take turns sitting and pushing up into your Side Plank. Swap sides and repeat.

393 Side Plank and Hip Raise with Feet on a Balance Ball

Come into a side forearm plank with your feet stacked at the center of your balance ball. Let your free hand rest on the hip. Take turns lowering and lifting the hips. This is an awesome exercise for stabilizing the lower back and core.

394 Side Plank with Hip and Leg Raise with Arm

By incorporating a balance ball, this plank variation works on stabilizing not only the core, but also the shoulder and rotator cuff! When working with an unstable surface, like the balance ball, your balance is challenged, giving you the opportunity to stabilize.

- Come into a side forearm plank with your left arm centered on your balance ball.
- Let your right hand rest on the hip.
- Press your hips up into a side plank and lift your right leg high up into the air.
- Bring the legs back together and lower the hips to the ground. Change sides and repeat.

395 Balance Ball Extended Arm Plank

Start with your balance ball flat side down. Bring your palms together with your arms extended, on top and in the center of the balance ball. Come into your plank by extending the legs long, putting the weight onto the balls of your feet.

396 Swiss Ball Shin Plank

Start with your shins propped up on the Swiss ball. Bring your palms to the floor and come into your plank by extending the legs long, balancing the weight onto your shins and hands. Squeeze the abs in tight.

397 Swiss Ball Plank with Leg Lift

Bring your body into an extended arm plank with your Swiss ball supporting your shins. Extend the legs long, and put the weight into your hands. Squeeze the abs in a lot and extend the spine forward while picking up the right leg. Keep your core tight as you alternate the legs.

398 Swiss Ball Forearm Plank

By incorporating a Swiss ball, this forearm plank variation works on stabilizing not only the core, but also the shoulder and rotator cuff! When working with a moving surface, your balance is challenged, giving you the opportunity to stabilize. Utilizing your Swiss ball as a moving prop for the lower body to manipulate, you will strengthen your abdominal wall and stabilize the pelvis.

- Place your forearms securely at the center of a Swiss ball. Place the balls of your feet on the floor.

- Activate your core deeply and bring your body to balance.

- Be sure to keep your body in one straight line from the top of the head to your heels. Keep your feet pressing into the floor, the legs long, and the abdominals pulling in.

399 Swiss Ball Loop Extension

Place a resistance band around your ankles and come into your forearm plank, centered on your Swiss ball. Extend the legs long and push the forearms strongly into the ball. Alternate lifting and lowering each leg up off of the floor, working against your band.

400 Swiss Ball Hand Walk-Around

Come into your long plank position with the arms fully extended. Stabilize at the hips and keep the lower body long in the air with the Swiss ball supporting your shins. Hold in your plank position, pull in the abs strongly, and move the hands to the right, then to the left, then lower down.

401 Swiss Ball Twist Walkaround

Bring your body into an extended plank with a Swiss ball under your knees. Squeeze the abs in, up, and away from the floor underneath you. Shift the hips open to the right and hold. Pull in the abs strongly, and alternate moving the hands to the right, then to the left.

402 Swiss Ball Hand Walk-Out

Come into your long plank position with the arms fully extended. Stabilize at the hips and keep the lower body long in the air with the Swiss ball supporting your knees and shins. Hold in your plank position, pull in the abs strongly, and alternate moving the hands out in front and then back toward the ball.

403 Swiss Ball Plank with In-Out

Come into an extended plank position with the tops of your feet at the center of the Swiss ball. Keeping your body in one straight line, tap the left foot out to the side of the ball, then the right. Step the right foot, then the left foot back up onto the ball. Repeat as many times as you can.

404

Swimming

Using your body's own weight, in this variation, to stretch the spine and engage the core and back muscles, creates length throughout the legs and torso. If you have wrist or elbow pain, making it difficult to balance or plank for long periods of time during your workout, this is a great variation for you.

- Lie face down on the floor with your arms stretched overhead and the legs long.
- Pull the abs up into the back, lift the right leg off the floor, and simultaneously reach the left arm forward.
- Alternate the arms and legs quickly up and down, reaching in opposing directions as if you were swimming.

Correct form
Pull the abdominals in. You should have them pulled up so deeply off the floor that there is space between the front of your abs and the ground.

Avoid
Do not let the muscles in your neck and upper shoulders pinch or tighten when performing your swimming.

Annotation Key
Bold text indicates target muscles
Black text indicates other working muscles
* indicates deep muscles

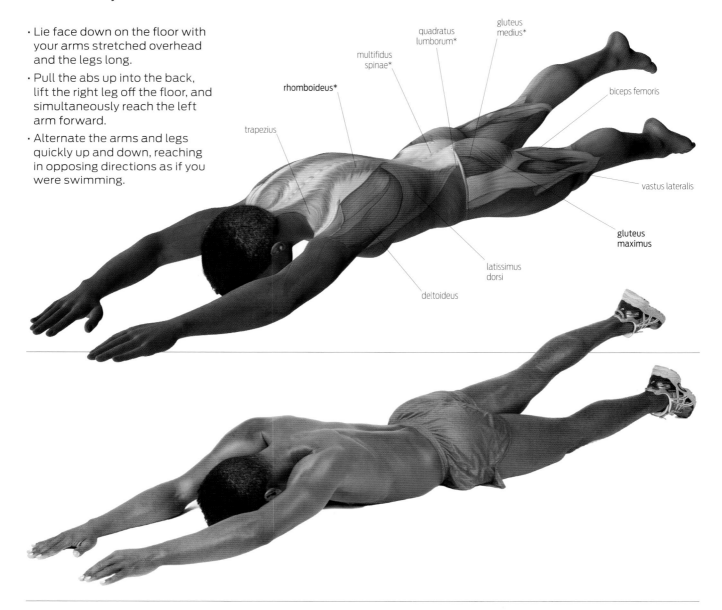

gluteus medius*

quadratus lumborum*

multifidus spinae*

rhomboideus*

trapezius

biceps femoris

vastus lateralis

gluteus maximus

latissimus dorsi

deltoideus

405 Superman

Extend your body long on top of a yoga mat. Bring your arms close together overhead and bring your legs to touch, squeezing the inner thighs tightly. Engage the abs strongly, and in one move lift your arms and legs off the floor together.

406 Prone Heel Beats

Balancing the body, isometrically, in one long shape while you focus on isolating the lower part of your legs—beating the heels—is a great way to work the legs and stabilize the core. In this heel beat variation you will work on keeping the body quiet and still while you move only the heels in towards each other.

- Begin lying with your face toward the floor.
- Squeeze your abdominals tightly, engage the backs of the legs, and raise the body up off the floor into a Superman shape.
- Bring your hands along your sides.
- Begin opening and closing the heels in toward each other and then out.

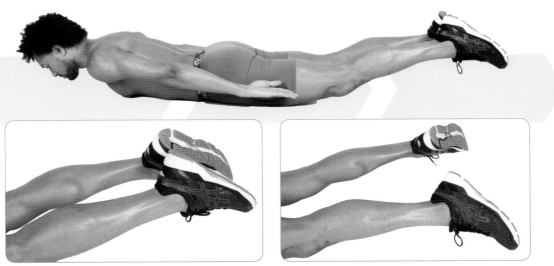

407 Advanced Superman

Lie face down along the floor. Bend your arms and bring your hands together at the base of your neck. Squeezing the inner thighs tightly, engage the abs strongly, and in one move lift your torso and legs off the floor together.

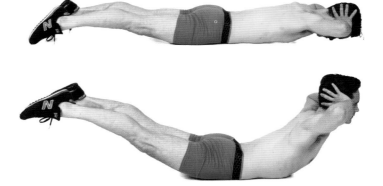

408 Weighted Superman

Perform your Advanced Superman (#407) holding a weighted ball. While lying long on the floor take a weighted ball into your hands. Reach the arms forward and the legs back, bringing both ends of your body up off the floor.

409 Extension Pass

In this variation you will work on similar body muscles as in your Superman, Prone Heel Beats, and Swimming. The idea is that you extend your body long, coming off the floor, and once you are fully extended you hold in that position while you pass a ball back and forth between your hands.

- Perform your Advanced Superman (#407) holding a weighted ball.
- While lying long on the floor take a weighted ball into your hands.
- Reach the arms forward and the legs back, bringing both ends of your body up off the floor.
- Once at the top of your shape, open the arms, and, begin passing your ball back and forth between your hands.

410 Face-Down Snow Angel

Extend your body long on top of a yoga mat. Bring your arms close together overhead and bring your legs to touch, squeezing the inner thighs tightly. Engage the abs strongly, and in one move lift your arms and legs off the floor together. Open your arms and legs to the side and hold here.

411 The Seal

Start sitting up with your feet on the floor and your back long and straight. Pick your legs up into a 90-degree angle and thread your arms under your calves, resting your hands on top of the upper ankles. Squeeze the abs in and the core tight, and allow the body to rock back into space, quickly recovering back up to your starting position and balancing there.

412 Balance Ball Superman

Lie face down with the Balance Ball underneath your abs. Bend your arms and bring your hands together at the base of your neck. Squeezing the inner thighs tightly, engage the abs strongly, and in one move lift your torso and legs off the floor together.

413 Prone Cobra

Extend your body long on top of a yoga mat. Bring your arms close together overhead and bring your legs to touch, squeezing the inner thighs tightly. Engage the abs strongly, and in one move lift your arms up behind you and the legs off the floor together.

414 Prone Trunk Raise

Extend your body long on top of a yoga mat. Bring your arms close to your sides, palms down and bring your legs to touch, squeezing the inner thighs tightly. Engage the abs strongly, and in one move push your upper body forward and up off the floor, coming into a high arch.

415 Arm Hauler

This variation is similar to the Prone Cobra. Bring your arms close together overhead and squeeze your legs tightly together. Engage the abs strongly, and in one move lift your arms back and to the sides and your legs off the floor together.

416 Bent Arm Towel Fly

Spread a small towel along the floor. Place your hands onto the towel at a shoulder-width distance. Come into your extended arm plank with the body long and abdominals engaged. Bend your arms, and as you lower push the hands on top of the towel in toward each other, then straighten your arms as you slide them apart.

417 Dive Bomber

Begin in a High Plank position (#366). Engage the core and bend at the hips coming onto your hands and feet in a downward dog shape. Bend the arms, push the hips forward, and dip the head down through the arms, coming into an upward high arch with the torso.

418 Prone Arm Raises

Lie face down on the floor with your arms stretched overhead and the legs long. Pull the abs up into the back. Reach the right arm forward off the floor and hold, then lower and reach the left arm.

419 Supine Flutter Kicks

Start lying on your back, with a very long and straight spine. Bring your arms to your sides, and extend the legs out long on a low diagonal. Alternate crossing one ankle over the other while holding your legs long.

420 Swiss Ball Rotated Back Extension

Working with the Swiss ball in this backwards crunch variation provides an unstable, soft surface for the lower back and core to stabilize on. Giving you an element of instability, the ball will help to develop balance in the core and lower back, as well as work deeper into your abdominals.

- Start lying face down, with the Swiss ball under your abdominals and hips.
- Bring your arms close together behind the back of the head, and bring your legs to a shoulder-width stance.
- Engage the abs strongly, and in one move lift your torso up off of the Swiss ball.
- Take a rotation to the right and then to the left, opening up each side of the body and working the obliques deeply.

421 Weighted Ball Heel Beats

Begin lying with your face towards the floor. Place a weighted ball under your pelvis, and squeeze your abdominals tightly. Engage the backs of the legs. Raise the body up off the floor into a forearm plank. Begin opening and closing the heels in toward each other and then out.

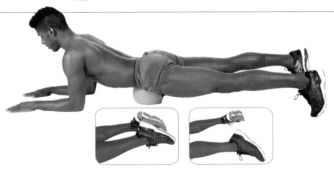

422 Balance Ball Back Extensions

Start laying face down, with the balance ball under your abdominals and hips. Bring your arms close together behind the back of the head, and bring your legs together. Engage the abs strongly, and in one move lift your torso up off of the ball, keeping your feet on the floor.

423 Balance Ball Shoulder Raise

Begin in a hip-width open stance on top of your balance ball. Open your arms wide to the sides, holding the dumbbells. Lift and lower the arms laterally. Keep the core squeezing in and the arms at chest height.

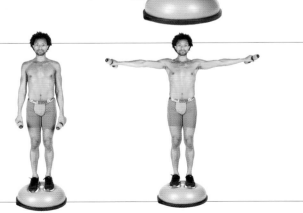

424

Side Passé

The word "passé" stems from the French classical ballet term meaning "to pass." Passé is a movement where you bring a pointed foot up high, along the inside of your leg, ending with the pointed foot and leg creating a sort of triangle shape at the side of the knee. In this Side Passé variation you will use the weight of the floor to help isolate the movement, creating stability in the pelvis and hip joints.

Correct form
This is a movement that calls for absolute stability. The less you move the better. Deeply engage your abs and only move one leg at a time.

Avoid
Do not let the hips push back or rock forward. Keep the hips stacked straight up and down, in line with your core and shoulders to the front.

Annotation Key
Bold text indicates target muscles
Black text indicates other working muscles
* indicates deep muscles

vastus medialis

biceps femoris

sartorius

adductor magnus

gluteus maximus

transversus abdominis*

adductor longus

vastus lateralis

rectus femoris

tensor fasciae latae

rectus abdominis

- Lie on your left side with the left arm supporting the head and the right arm out in front of your chest for balance.
- Extend the left leg long and stack the right leg on top of it.
- Trace the right foot up along the inside of the left leg.
- Once your foot reaches the knee, isolate the lower part of the right leg and extend it open and up to the right side. Repeat on the other side.

425 Side Lift Bend

Begin lying on the right side of your body. Place your right hand behind your head and extend your left arm long. With the feet flexed, squeeze the abs in, lift the legs, and crunch into the left side of your abdominals. Lower, and repeat before changing sides.

426 Kneeling Side Lift

Kneel with the weight balanced on both knees. Place the hands behind the head and shift your weight onto the right side. Extend your left leg long out from the hip. Press the hips forward, lift the abdominals up, and kick the left leg up off the ground. Swap sides and repeat.

427 Upper Body Lift Bend

Begin lying on the right side of your body. Place your right hand behind your head and extend your left arm long. With the feet flexed, squeeze the abs in, lift the side of the body, and crunch into the left side of your abdominals. Lower and repeat, then change sides.

428 Clamshell Series

Begin lying on the left side of your body. Place your left forearm down on the floor, propping your upper body up. Bring the knees into a right angle behind your hips, and flex the feet. Squeeze the abs in, lift the heels up, and open the knees. Lower and repeat, then change sides.

429 Side Lying Hip Abduction

Begin lying on the right side of your body. Place your right hand behind your head and place your left hand on the hip. Squeeze the core into your back and pull the left leg out away from your hips, raising it up into the air to hip height. Lower back down and repeat. Swap sides.

430

Oblique Roll-Down

Correct form
While performing your Roll-Down take care to keep the legs squeezing in toward each other, as well as engaging the abs.

Avoid
Do not allow the shoulders to rise up to the ears. Keep them pinned down and into the middle back.

This variation of core exercise can be found in almost all abdominal-focused workouts like yoga, Pilates, ballet barre, and calisthenics. The focus is on keeping the core stabilized in a seated position while you twist to either side, slowly rolling the spine down, piece by piece. Doing this move will not only stabilize the core, but also create stability and strength in the pelvis and lower back.

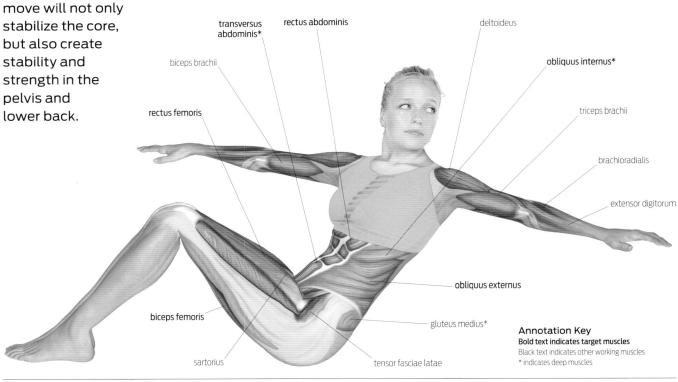

transversus abdominis*

rectus abdominis

deltoideus

biceps brachii

obliquus internus*

rectus femoris

triceps brachii

brachioradialis

extensor digitorum

obliquus externus

biceps femoris

gluteus medius*

sartorius

tensor fasciae latae

Annotation Key
Bold text indicates target muscles
Black text indicates other working muscles
* indicates deep muscles

- Start sitting up with your knees slightly bent.
- Bring the bottoms of your feet to the floor.
- Open your arms wide so that your body is facing flat to the front.
- Rotate from your obliques to the left, keep the arms open, and roll the body down to the floor. Swap sides and repeat.

431 Rolling Like a Ball

Start sitting. Pick your legs up into a 90-degree angle and thread your arms around your thighs to hold the backs of the knees. Squeeze the abs in and the core tight, and allow the body to rock back into space, quickly recovering back up to your starting position and balancing there.

432 Roll-Down

Begin lying down in your standard Sit-Up starting position. Bring your legs together and your arms to your sides. Engage the core muscles and squeeze your lower abdominals into the back. Reach the arms forward and off the floor, coming into a seated position. Roll down and repeat.

433 Half Curl

Lie on the ground with your knees bent, feet flat in the floor, and arms by your sides. Engage your abs, tuck your chin into your chest, and curl your body up just until your upper back comes off the floor.

434 Neck Pull

The Neck Pull is a movement that originates from Pilates workouts. This is the beginner version. The Neck Pull is a kind of "Roll-Out" that is excellent for building up those deep inner core muscles that provide stability for your lower back. Neck Pulls are also excellent for improving posture, balance, and reducing back pain.

- Begin lying down on your back with your body long and straight.
- Bring your legs together and your hands behind your head to support your neck.
- Engage the core muscles and squeeze your lower abdominals into the back. Reach the torso forward and off the floor, articulating through each part of the spine.

435

Jackknife

The Jackknife is a very challenging move that is used in both Pilates and yoga routines. Pulling the legs up overhead from a low extended body position requires abdominal power, balance, and a supple spine. Adding this exercise into your daily workouts will increase core strength and stability throughout the spine, and will help soothe the nervous system by bringing the body upside down.

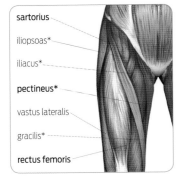

sartorius
iliopsoas*
iliacus*
pectineus*
vastus lateralis
gracilis*
rectus femoris

Correct form
You should aim to have your entire upper, middle, and lower back flush with the floor underneath you before picking up the body into the elevated position.

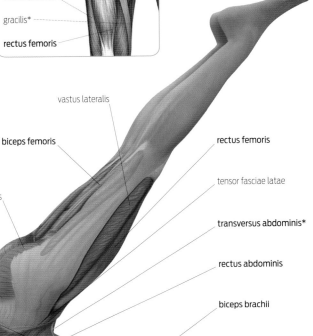

vastus lateralis

biceps femoris

gluteus maximus

gluteus medius*

obliquus externus

obliquus internus*

brachioradialis

extensor digitorum

rectus femoris

tensor fasciae latae

transversus abdominis*

rectus abdominis

biceps brachii

triceps brachii

deltoideus

Annotation Key
Bold text indicates target muscles
Black text indicates other working muscles
* indicates deep muscles

Avoid
Do not drop the legs so low past the point of being able to keep the abdominals pulling into the body while lying long on the floor.

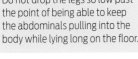

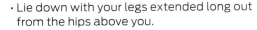

- Lie down with your legs extended long out from the hips above you.
- Scoop the lower abdominals and lower the legs down with your feet pointed.
- Keeping your back flat along the floor, and the hips still, pull the abs in and lift the legs up, then the hips, then the back, up and over the top of your head. Keep the trajectory of your legs pulling up toward the ceiling.
- Slowly, control the lowering down of your spine as you return to the starting position.

436 Corkscrew

Lie down with your legs extended long out from the hips above you. Scoop the lower abdominals and lower the legs down to a 45-degree angle. Engage the legs and core and press your legs together to the left side. Sweep them down to just off of the floor at low center, and lift them to the right, then sweeping up to high center as you began.

437 Scissors

Lie with the body extending long on the floor. Pull in your lower abdominals, reach the arms forward, and come into a long-legged crunch. Lift the legs off the floor and reach the left leg high up toward the chest. Reach with both arms and pull the left leg in closer to your chest. Switch legs and pull the right.

438 Double Leg Ab Press

When you balance with your knees up past hip height you are engaging your core deeply. Simultaneously, you are giving the lower back a stretch down through the hamstring. Holding the knees up into the chest in this exercise, while pressing against them from your core, will activate your obliques and lower back muscles.

- With your spine along the floor, bring the arms to your sides.
- Squeeze your legs together in a 90-degree shape, out in front of your hips.
- Come into a Sit-Up and engage the abs tightly.
- Use both of your hands to press against your quads as you sit up higher toward the knees.

439 V-Up

Start lying flat on your back with your legs long and extended. Hold your arms overhead to begin. Pull the legs forward and up off the floor as you reach your arms long, out further from the top of your head.

440 Straight Leg Raise

Extend the legs out long from the hips above you. Scoop the lower abdominals and lower the legs down with your feet flexed. Keeping your chest and hips still, pull the abs in again and lift the legs back up.

441 Open Leg Rocker

It is very important to keep your abdominals pulled up and squeezing into your spine when performing your Pilates variations of Rolling Like a Ball, the Seal, and this Open Leg Rocker. Any sort of arch or hyperextension in the lower back could lead to strain and back pain.

- Start sitting. Pick your legs up into a slight V-shape.
- Reach your hands for your feet and hold tightly around the ankles.
- Squeeze the abs in and engage the core tightly.
- Allow the body to rock back into space, coming to roll onto the middle back.
- Quickly recover back up to your starting position and balance there.
- Repeat, increasing the distance between your feet each time.

442 Lemon Squeezer

Begin with the body flat on the floor. Place your hands behind your lower back, and bend your left leg in. Engage your lower abdominals deeply and come up into a crunch. Take care to not push yourself up with your hands—only let the core do the work. Repeat on the other side.

443 The Criss-Cross

Bend your legs and bring them together at a 90-degree angle from your hips. Come up into your crunch position and hold there. Extend your right leg out parallel with the floor and rotate the upper body towards the left raised leg, bringing your left knee into the chest. Swap sides.

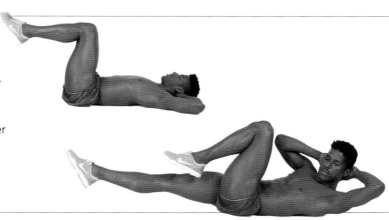

444 Hundred 1

The Hundred is a movement that originates from Pilates workouts. This is the beginner version. Begin lying down in your standard Sit-Up position. Bring your legs together and your arms to your sides. Squeeze your lower abdominals into the back, reach the arms forward and off the floor, and come into your crunch. Hold.

445 Hundred 2

Start in your standard Sit-Up position. Bring your legs together and your arms to your sides. Engage the core muscles and elevate the legs off the floor into a right angle. Reach the arms forward and off the floor and crunch into your abs. Hold.

446 Teaser 1

Lie down with your legs floating at a 90-degree angle from the hips above you. Scoop the lower abdominals and lengthen the legs into the air with your feet pointed. Reach the arms forward along the legs, coming up into a high V-shape with the legs raised.

447 Teaser 2

This double leg, beautifully simple Teaser II variation gives you the opportunity to work the deep inner core muscles, which can be hard to reach sometimes. By keeping the legs elevated in the air and stabilizing from deep inside your core, you will strengthen both internal and external abdominal groups.

- Lie down with your legs floating long out from the hips above you.
- Scoop the lower abdominals, lower the legs, and raise the arms overhead.
- Keeping your back flat along the floor, and the hips still, pull the abs in again and reach the arms forward along the legs, coming up into a high V-shape with the legs raised.

448 Balance Ball Seated Leg Tucks

Sit toward the edge of a balance ball with the flat side flush on the floor. The balance ball gives you an added element of balance and supports the lower back. Pull your knees in to meet your chest, and then extend them out in front of you. Keep your abs engaged the whole time.

449 Balance Ball Single Leg Ab Extension

Lie with the balance ball supporting your upper back. Bend your legs and bring them together at a 90-degree angle from your hips. Come up into your crunch position and hold there. Extend your right leg out and lift the upper body towards the left raised leg. Alternate sides and repeat.

450 Swiss Ball Lying Leg Rotation

Lie down with your legs extended long out from the hips above you. Place the Swiss ball between your legs and scoop the lower abdominals. Lower the legs down with your feet pointed, and alternate rotating the ball from side to side. Keeping your back flat along the floor, and the hips still, pull the abs in again and lift the legs back up.

451 Swiss Ball Jackknife

Begin in your plank position with the arms fully extended. Walk your feet up onto the Swiss ball. Squeeze the abs up and in and and pull your knees toward the chest on the ball. Slowly extend back out and repeat.

CHAPTER THREE

Core Yoga Exercises

The physical body is divided into two sections: the upper half and the lower half. The upper body contains the head, neck, shoulders, chest, back body muscle groups, front of the body abdominal groups, and all of our organs. And the lower abdominals and spine, pelvis, thighs, glutes, knees, calves, ankles, and feet encompass the glorious lower body. The art and practice of yoga strives to incorporate total balance within these two portions of the body, as well as throughout the metaphysical and spiritual parts that make up each of us. Combining yoga into your workout gives you an opportunity to focus on the use of your breath within your core work. Breathing, stretching, and visualizing are all vital components that will make your yoga practice more enriching and successful.

Warrior I

Warrior I is a beginning movement that you will certainly move through, should you find yourself in a yoga class one day. Holding your Warrior I pose will give you all sorts of isometric exercise benefits. This stance is a balanced position in which you open your legs wide, reach the arms high above the head, suck the abdominals in, deeply bend your front knee, and use your gaze to look forward. It incorporates elements of lunging with stretching.

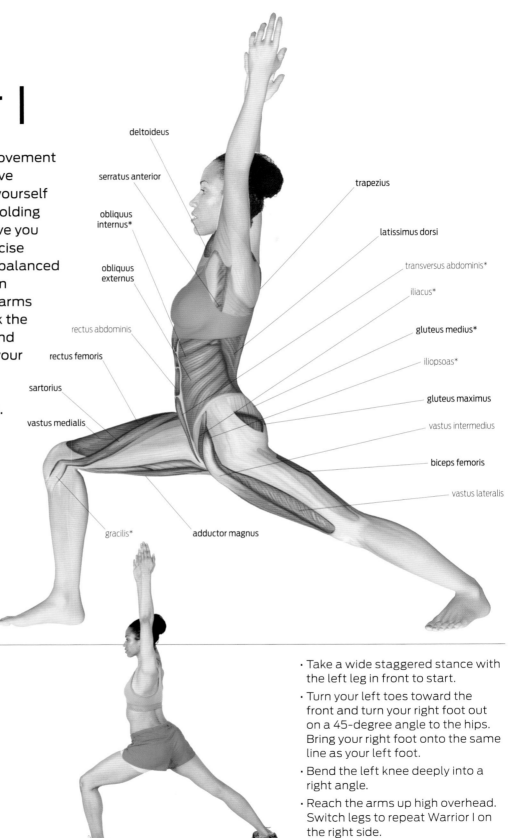

deltoideus

serratus anterior

obliquus internus*

obliquus externus

rectus abdominis

rectus femoris

sartorius

vastus medialis

gracilis*

adductor magnus

trapezius

latissimus dorsi

transversus abdominis*

iliacus*

gluteus medius*

iliopsoas*

gluteus maximus

vastus intermedius

biceps femoris

vastus lateralis

Annotation Key
Bold text indicates target muscles
Black text indicates other working muscles
* indicates deep muscles

Correct form
Be sure to keep the abdominals long and the lower back straight. Keep your gaze forward past the front of the chest.

Avoid
Do not let the front knee bend past 90 degrees. Make sure your bent knee is in alignment with your front foot.

- Take a wide staggered stance with the left leg in front to start.
- Turn your left toes toward the front and turn your right foot out on a 45-degree angle to the hips. Bring your right foot onto the same line as your left foot.
- Bend the left knee deeply into a right angle.
- Reach the arms up high overhead. Switch legs to repeat Warrior I on the right side.

453 Bound Warrior

Take a wide staggered stance with the right leg in front to start. Turn your right toes toward the front and turn your left foot out on a 45-degree angle to the hips. Bend the right knee deeply into a right angle. Reach down and wrap your right arm under the right thigh and thread the left arm behind the back to touch the right hand on the thigh. Swap sides and repeat.

454 Warrior I Backbend

Take your deep staggered Warrior I stance with the right leg forward. Arch up and back, bringing your gaze behind your right shoulder. Place your left hand on the back of the left knee, and reach the right arm back behind the head, bringing the thumb and index finger to touch. Swap sides and repeat.

455 Warrior I Open Chest Hands Bound

This variation of Warrior I is excellent for stabilizing the legs while gaining a deep front of the body opening stretch. Arching back into space with the abdominals, chest, and neck exposed open to the sky is an intense opening stretch for both the front and back of the body.

- Take your deep staggered Warrior I stance with the right leg forward.
- Interlace your fingers and arch up and back.
- Bend your right knee deeply and stretch your arms up behind you, continuing the reach into your back arch.
- Bring your focus onto a point behind the body. Repeat with the left leg forward.

456 Bowing Reverse Prayer Warrior

Take a wide staggered stance with the left leg in front to start. Bring your hands behind the back, and place the fingertips of the hands and then the palms into a reverse prayer position behind the middle back. Bend the left knee, rotate the torso open to the right, and bring your left shoulder to the inside of your left knee. Switch sides and repeat.

457 Hand Position of Cow Face Pose

Start with the legs open wide to the sides. Reach the right arm up overhead and reach the left arm down. Bend both elbows so the hands come to touch behind the back. Take a side lunge with the right knee bent deeply and bring the top of your head to the floor in front. Swap sides and repeat.

458 Reverse Warrior

Take your deep staggered Warrior I stance with the right leg forward. Arch up and back, bringing your gaze behind your right shoulder. Place your left hand on the back of the left calf, and reach the right arm back behind the head. Repeat on the other side.

459 Tiptoe Warrior

Take your deep staggered Warrior I stance with the right leg forward. Arch up and back, bringing your gaze behind your right shoulder and raising the right heel off the floor. Reach your left hand forward with your thumb and index finger touching, and reach the right arm back behind the head with the thumb and finger touching also. Swap sides and repeat.

460 Warrior II

Take a wide staggered stance with the right leg in front. Turn your right toes toward the front and turn your left foot out to a 45-degree angle. Bend the right knee deeply into a 90-degree angle. Reach the right arm forward and the left arm back, all in one line. Swap sides and repeat.

461 Bound Revolved Son of Anjani

Open the legs very wide and bend the left knee deeply into a right angle. Open the arms to the front. Rotate the torso to the left and reach the left elbow outside of the left thigh, bringing your right forearm under the left thigh. Reach the left arm behind your back, above your right hip and bring the left and right hands together into a bind. Raise the right heel. Swap sides and repeat.

462 Revolved Son of Anjani in Prayer

This prayer pose is simply a hold of your deep lunge. It requires lots of balance and the ability to rotate the torso deeply so that you may bring the hands into a prayer pose against the opposing bent knee. Keeping your focus in one place is important for a successful balance.

- Open the legs very wide and bend the left knee deeply into a right angle.
- Open the arms to the front and rotate the torso to the left.
- Bend forward at the hips and bring your right forearm under your left knee.
- Bring the left hand on top of the right hand, coming into a prayer shape. Repeat with the right leg forward.

463 Fighting Warrior II

Stagger your legs open wide with the right leg in front. Bend the right knee into a right angle and bend the back left leg into one as well. Rotate the torso open to the left and place the right elbow onto the right knee, extending the left arm up on the diagonal. Repeat with the left leg in front.

464 Bowing Warrior II

Open the legs very wide and bend the left knee deeply into a right angle. Open the arms to the front and bring your hands to clasp behind your hips. Bend forward deeply from the hips and bring your head to the inside of your left foot. Un-clasp the hands, sweep your left arm under your left thigh, and re-clasp your hands around your left knee. Swap sides and repeat.

465 Bowing Warrior II with Raised Bound Hands

This deeply bowing Warrior II pose is great for stretching the hamstrings, calves, lower back, and shoulders. If you are finding it challenging to bind the hands behind you, it is perfectly acceptable to perform this move with the hands on the hips.

- Start standing with the legs open wide to the sides.
- Clasp the hands behind the back.
- Bend forward deeply in the hips, bringing your head to the center of the floor between your legs.
- Take a side lunge, bending the left knee. Alternate hand clasping and switch sides.

466 Warrior III

Take a wide staggered stance with the left leg forward. Turn your left toes toward the front and turn your right foot out to a 45-degree angle. Bend the left knee deeply into a 90-degree angle. Reach the arms up overhead. Push off the right foot, bend the torso forward, and straighten both legs. Swap sides.

467 Warrior Arms at Sides

Take a wide staggered stance with the left leg forward. Turn your left toes toward the front and turn your right foot out to a 45-degree angle. Bend the left knee deeply into a 90-degree angle. Reach the arms up overhead. Push off the right foot, bend the torso forward, and straighten both legs. Reach the arms toward your right foot with the thumbs and index fingers touching. Repeat on the other side.

468 Warrior Reverse Prayer

Take a wide staggered stance with the left leg forward. Bend the left knee deeply into a 90-degree angle. Reach the arms behind the back into your reverse prayer position. Push off the right foot, bend the torso forward, and straighten both legs. Balance here. Swap sides and repeat.

469 Half Moon

Take a wide staggered stance with the left leg forward. Bend the left knee deeply and come into your Warrior I stance with the arms reaching overhead. Spin the left hand to the floor, about 2 feet (60 cm) in front of the left foot. Push off the right foot and come to balance on your left foot and left hand. Lift the right leg high and extend the right arm up towards the leg. Repeat on the other side.

470 Half Lotus

Start standing tall. Using your left hand, bring your right foot high up onto the front of the left thigh and hold it there. Reach the right arm up overhead. Bend forward from the hips, lift the right foot up higher into the hip, and bring both hands forward into extended prayer. Repeat on the other side.

471 One Leg Stretched Upward

Start in your Warrior I position (#452) with the arms up overhead and the right knee bent. Reach the arms forward and place them on the floor far in front of the right foot. Push off the left leg and extend your left leg high up into the air. Repeat with the right leg raised.

472 Bowing with One Leg Stretched Upward

Start in your Warrior I position (#452) with the arms up overhead and the left knee bent. Reach the arms forward and place them on the floor, one either side of the left foot, bending the left knee slightly. Push off the right leg, bring the torso close to the left shin, and extend your right leg high up into the air. Swap sides and repeat.

473 Unsupported One Leg

Start in your Warrior I position (#452) with the arms up overhead and the left knee bent. Reach the arms forward and place them on either side of the left foot. Push off the right leg and extend your right leg high up into the air. When you have found your balance, reach your left arm up towards your right toes, and then reach the right arm too! Swap sides and repeat.

474 Bowing with Respect Pose

This Bowing with Respect Pose is on the more advanced end of yoga poses. If you can manage it, you will give yourself a deep amount of stretch throughout the legs, as well as through the arms and shoulders via your bind. Also, finding and holding this balance is great for stabilizing the core and pelvis. Good luck and do not forget to breathe.

- Stand long on your left leg and bend your right leg into Tree Pose, bringing the bottom of the right foot to rest on the inside of the left knee.
- Reach your right hand down to hold the right toes.
- With the right hand, open the right leg to the side. Switch the grip from the toes to the back of the upper right ankle.
- Place the left hand on your hip and take a deep bend forward from the hips, bringing your back onto the diagonal.
- Thread the left arm around the lower back to rest in the right front hip crease.
- Change your right hand grip and press against the right leg, pushing it up high with the right hand. Swap sides and repeat.

Keeping Your Balance

In all yoga positions, balances, stretches, binds, and meditations, it is of deep importance to find your focus, both internally and externally. In order to find a proper balance, you must find a focus for it first. This means, literally, finding a point in front of you or in the direction of your balance that you keep your eyes fixed on, no matter what. Keep your focus clear and keep breathing. You can do it!

475 Basic Bowing with Respect Pose

Stand long on your left leg and bend your right leg into Tree Pose, bringing the bottom of the right foot to rest on the inside of the left knee. Reach your right hand down to hold the right toes. With the right hand, open the right leg to the side. Bend forward from the hips, bringing your back onto the diagonal. Thread the left arm around the lower back to rest in the right front hip crease. Change your right hand grip and press against the right leg, pushing it sideways with the right hand. Swap legs and repeat.

476 Bowing with Respect Bird of Paradise

Come into your Bowing with Respect Pose (#475), either the beginner or advanced version. Bring your left hand from your right hip crease onto your left hip. Bend your right leg slightly, and place your right arm far underneath your right knee, straightening your arm and bringing your right thumb and index finger to touch. Extend your left arm out to the left with the same finger placement. Swap sides.

477

Bound Angle Pose

The Bound Angle Pose is a restful, restorative position to take in your yoga workout routine. It allows you to sit with both legs, feet, and arms in proportionate balance, keeping your back and torso long and fluid. If you'd like more of a stretch in this pose, bring your hands to the tops of your thighs and push down.

Correct form

You want both sides of the body to be in proportion to each other. The knees, legs, and feet should all be in equal alignment to your torso.

Avoid

Do not force your legs to the floor if you are tight. Also, allow space between your feet and hips if that is comfortable for you. If you are having trouble sitting on the floor, place a cushion or block underneath your hips.

Annotation Key
Bold text indicates target muscles
Black text indicates other working muscles
* indicates deep muscles

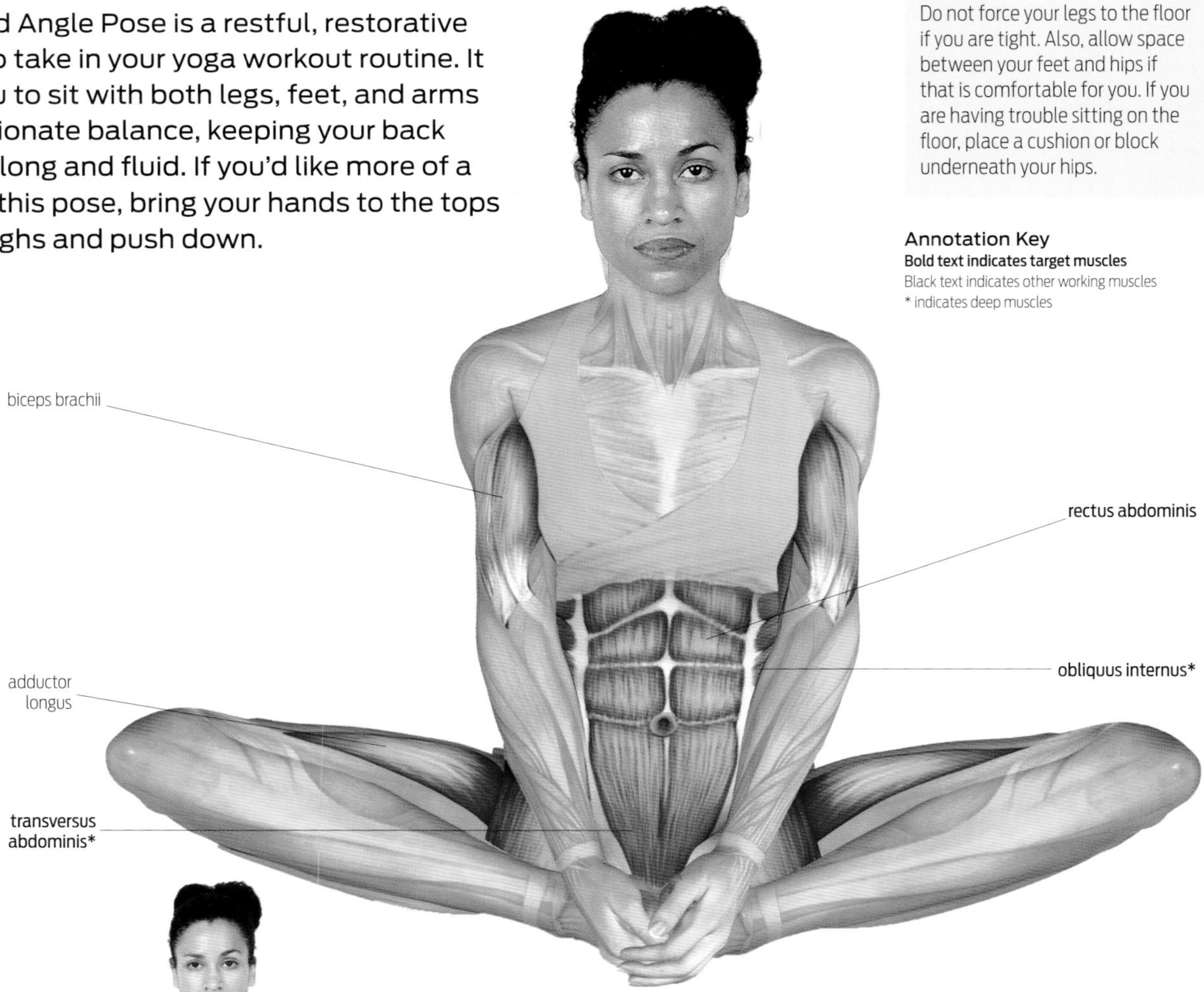

biceps brachii
rectus abdominis
obliquus internus*
adductor longus
transversus abdominis*

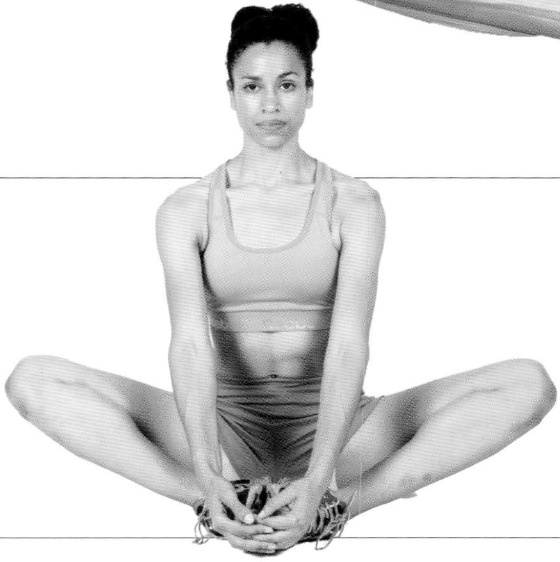

- Come to sit on your behind with your back nice and long.
- Bring the soles of your feet together, about 1 to 2 feet (30 to 60 cm) away from the front of your hips.
- Clasp your hands around your toes and use your inner thigh muscles to push down on your legs, bringing the outer legs close to the floor for a stretch.

478 Bound Angle Pose with Hands in Prayer

Come to sit on your behind with your back nice and long. Bring the soles of your feet together, about 1 to 2 feet (30 to 60 cm) away from the front of your hips. Place your hands together in front of the chest. Take a curve forward from the head, and rest here.

479 Bound Angle Pose Bending Forward

Come to sit on your behind with your back nice and long. Bring the soles of your feet together, about 1 to 2 feet (30 to 60 cm) away from the front of your hips. Clasp your hands around your toes and use your arms to pull your chest forward and close to your feet.

480 Bound Hands Bound Angle Pose

This variation of Bound Angle Pose is deeply meditative. Take your time in this pose to allow the heart and chest to open towards the front, allowing the back muscles to rest long against the spine. Engage the core muscles to lengthen the front of the body as you sit and restore the body.

- Come to sit on your behind with your back tall and long.
- Bring the soles of your feet together, about 1 to 2 feet (30 to 60 cm) away from the front of your hips.
- Place your hands behind your hips, bend at each elbow, and reach each opposing hand to hold the opposite elbow.

Relax and Restore

There are some yoga poses that call for you to simply relax. Yoga comprises all sorts of challenging poses and movements, so to balance these out there are a myriad of restorative shapes. If you do not practice yoga, you can still use these serene meditative poses, such as Bound Hands Bound Angle Pose, to close your eyes, breathe deeply, and find some peace. If the shape on the floor is not relaxing for you, grab a pillow or yoga block, and place it under your hips to elevate your position.

481 Reverse Prayer Bound Angle Pose

Come to sit with your back tall and long. Bring the soles of your feet together, about 1 to 2 feet (30 to 60 cm) away from the front of your hips. Place your hands behind your hips, bend at each elbow, and come into a reverse prayer position with the arms behind the back.

482 Hand Position of the Cow Face in Bound Angle Pose

Come to sit with your back tall and long. Bring the soles of your feet together, about 1 to 2 feet (30 to 60 cm) away from the front of your hips. Reach the right arm up overhead and reach the left arm down. Bend both elbows so that the hands come to touch behind the back. Swap hand positions and repeat.

483 Sideways Bound Angle Pose

Come to sit with your back tall and long. Bring the soles of your feet together, about 1 to 2 feet (30 to 60 cm) away from the front of your hips. Place the left arm behind your left hip and place the right hand on top of the right thigh and press gently down on it. Turn the gaze to the sky. Change sides and repeat.

484 Equilibrium Bound Angle Pose

Come to sit with your back tall and long. Bring the soles of your feet together, about 1 to 2 feet (30 to 60 cm) away from the front of your hips. Clasp the hands around both of your feet and rock your weight back toward your lower back, bringing the feet to float off the floor.

485

Bound Angle Pose Reaching Forward

Come to sit with your back tall and long. Bring the soles of your feet together, about 1 to 2 feet (30 to 60 cm) away from the front of your hips. Reach both arms forward and stretch the lower back while you curve the upper spine.

486

Bound Angle Pose Chin to Floor

Come to sit with your back tall and long. Bring the soles of your feet together, about 1 to 2 feet (30 to 60 cm) away from the front of your hips. Allow the legs to cross slightly and tip your weight forward, placing your hands down onto the floor. Extend your chin long on the floor and bring your hands in to the chest.

487

Bound Angle Pose Prayer Hands

This is another position that allows you to stretch the lower back forward against the legs in a seated position. Take care to really reach the arms far out in front of you before you come into your final prayer shape. Breathe deeply in this pose.

- Come to sit on your behind with your back nice and long.
- Bring the soles of your feet together, about 1 to 2 feet (30 to 60 cm) away from the front of your hips.
- Reach the arms long out to the front and bring them together in a prayer pose, with the head bowed into the floor.

488

Chaturanga

Chaturanga is an ancient Sanskrit term that is also known as a four-limbed staff pose or a low plank. It is, essentially, a moving plank pose that comes into a Push-Up. Traditionally, in a yoga class you would repeat this move with every sun salutation that you do, moving through at least 20 per class. Performing the Chaturanga is sure to give you a sculpted pair of arms and strong abdominals.

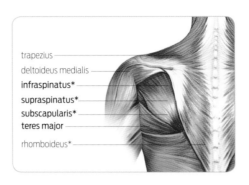

trapezius
deltoideus medialis
infraspinatus*
supraspinatus*
subscapularis*
teres major
rhomboideus*

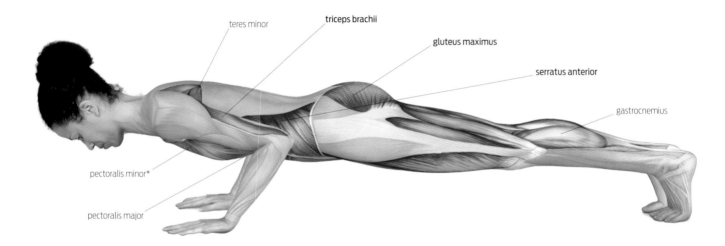

teres minor · triceps brachii · gluteus maximus · serratus anterior · gastrocnemius · pectoralis minor* · pectoralis major

Correct form
Squeeze the legs together and pull in your abs. Imagine you are an arrow shooting straight out from the space behind you.

Avoid
Try not to arch the back in this exercise by sinking in the abs. Pull in that core!

Annotation Key
Bold text indicates target muscles
Black text indicates other working muscles
* indicates deep muscles

- Start in an extended arm plank position.
- Pull the abdominals into the lower back.
- Bend the elbows, isolating them into the sides of the body. Hug the elbows in deeply to your sides.
- Hover in this position and move into lowering your chest to the floor once you fatigue.

489 One Arm Four-Limbed Staff Pose

Come onto your hands and knees with the arms extended straight. Squeeze in your abdominals and bring your left hand to the right inner arm. Let the weight of your body shift forward into the right hand. Swap sides and repeat.

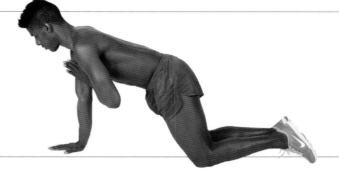

490 Revolved Four-Limbed Staff Pose

Lie on the left side of the body with the feet stacked on top of each other. Turn the torso to the floor, keeping the hips forward, legs stacked. Place the palms on either side of the shoulders and turn your head to the left. Swap sides.

491 One-Legged Four-Limbed Staff Pose

Bring your body into an extended arm plank. Extend the legs long, and put the weight onto the balls of your feet. Squeeze the abs in a lot and extend the spine forward while raising the right leg. Bend at the elbows and lower the body until the elbows hug into your sides. Swap sides.

492 Upward One Leg to the Side Staff Pose

Bring your body into an extended arm plank. Extend the legs long, and put the weight onto the balls of your feet. Bend at the elbows and lower the body until the elbows hug into your sides. Extend the spine forward, raise the right leg, and open it to the right side. Swap sides.

493 One Hand Four-Limbed Staff Pose

Bring your body into an extended arm plank. Extend the legs long, and put the weight onto the balls of your feet. Squeeze the abs in and extend the spine forward. Raise the right hand and bring it to the inside of your left arm. Balance on the left arm and two feet. Swap hands.

Headstand

Headstands are an advanced part of yoga. Once you are able to work yourself into a proper Headstand, you will be happy you did so. Performing Headstands stimulates and provides a fresh flow of blood via the heart into and throughout the entire body. Executing a good Headstand is also great for stretching the legs away from gravity, releasing toxins in the muscles.

- Begin kneeling on the floor with your shins flush with the ground.
- Bend forward and place your forearms down on the floor about a foot and a half (45 cm) from the fronts of your knees. Clasp the hands together to create a solid base.
- Open your forearms, giving yourself space to place your head down in between the arms.
- Place the top of the head up against your clasped palms and push the base of the hands against the back of the head.
- Straighten your legs and walk them in so that your torso is straight up over your head between your arms.
- Slowly bend your right leg up and then the left. Come to balance here. Extend the legs long overhead when you feel ready.

Correct form
Be sure that your foundation of forearms and hands are in a secure place. It is the base of your inversion.

Avoid
If you are a beginner head-stander do not attempt a Headstand without a wall to support you, at first.

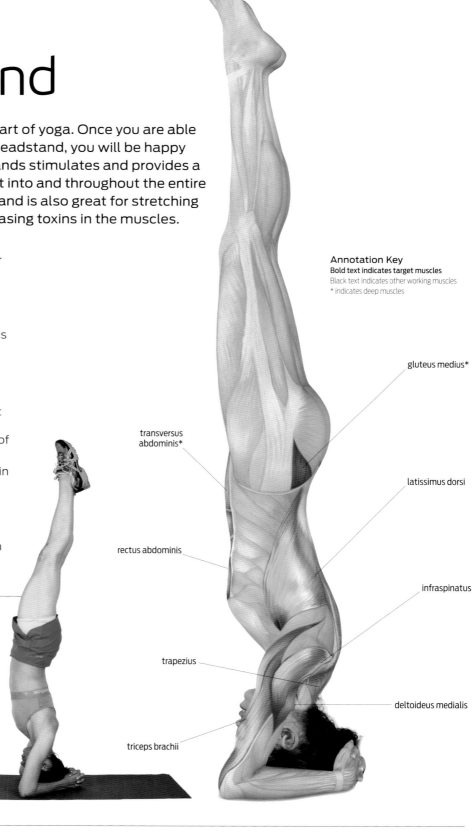

Annotation Key
Bold text indicates target muscles
Black text indicates other working muscles
* indicates deep muscles

gluteus medius*

transversus abdominis*

latissimus dorsi

rectus abdominis

infraspinatus

trapezius

deltoideus medialis

triceps brachii

495 One-Legged Headstand I

Come into your basic Headstand (#494), with the legs extended long. Hold your balance at the top, and engage the core deeply, keeping the weight over your head and arms. Slowly lower your left leg, bringing your toe to the floor in front of you and extending the right leg long overhead. Swap legs and repeat.

496 Leg Contraction Knee Bend Pose in Handstand

Come into your basic Headstand (#494), with the legs extended long. Hold your balance at the top, and engage the core deeply, keeping the weight over your head and arms. Slowly lower your right leg, bringing your toes behind your body and bend the left knee up toward the chest. Switch legs and repeat.

497 Auspicious Legs in Headstand

Come into your basic Headstand (#494), with the legs extended long. Hold your balance at the top, and engage the core deeply, keeping the weight over your head and arms. Slowly bend both knees open into a double stag shape in the air. Swap legs and repeat.

498 Seated Angle Pose in Headstand I

Come into your basic Headstand (#494), with the legs extended long. Hold your balance at the top, and engage the core deeply, keeping the weight over your head and arms. Slowly, open both of your legs straight out to either side of the body—attempt a split if you feel comfortable.

499 Bound Angle Pose in Headstand I

Come into your basic Headstand (#494), with the legs extended long. Hold your balance at the top, and engage the core deeply, keeping the weight over your head and arms. Slowly, bend both knees open to the sides and bring the soles of the feet together.

500 Half Auspicious Legs in Headstand

Come into your basic Headstand (#494), with the legs extended long. Hold your balance at the top, and engage the core deeply, keeping the weight over your head and arms. Slowly, lower your right leg, bringing the leg behind your body and bending the left knee up toward the chest. Switch legs and repeat.

501 Feet Spread Intense Stretch Pose in Headstand

Open the legs very wide and extend the arms long out to your sides. Bend at the hips and come forward into a flat angled shape. Bring the top of your head to the center of your legs, onto the floor. Bring the arms in together, pressing the forearms tightly together, and opening the fingers to stand on their tips in front of your face on the floor.

Index of Exercises

Credits

Photography

Naila Ruechel

Photography Assistant

Finn Moore

Models

Natasha Diamond-Walker
Abdiel Jacobson
Jessica Gambellur
Philip Chan
Anzie Dasabe
Lloyd Knight
Roya Carreras
Alex Geissbuhler
Daniel Wright

Additional Photography

Page 7 Undrey/Shutterstock.com
Page 9 bbernard/Shutterstock.com
Page 10; 16–17 Jacob Lund/Shutterstock.com
Pages 116–117 g-stockstudio/Shutterstock.com
Pages 168–169 fizkes/Shutterstock.com

Illustration

All anatomical illustrations by Hector Diaz/3DLabz Animation Limited

Full-body anatomy and Insets by Linda Bucklin/Shutterstock.com